New Directions for Community Colleges

Arthur M. Cohen
EDITOR-IN-CHIEF

Richard L. Wagoner
ASSOCIATE EDITOR

Allison Kanny
MANAGING EDITOR

Implementing Transfer Associate Degrees: Perspectives from the States

Carrie B. Kisker
Richard L. Wagoner
EDITORS

Number 160 • Winter 2012
Jossey-Bass
San Francisco

IMPLEMENTING TRANSFER ASSOCIATE DEGREES: PERSPECTIVES FROM THE STATES
Carrie B. Kisker and Richard L. Wagoner (eds.)
New Directions for Community Colleges, no. 160

Arthur M. Cohen, Editor-in-Chief
Richard L. Wagoner, Associate Editor
Allison Kanny, Managing Editor

Copyright © 2013 Wiley Periodicals, Inc., A Wiley Company. All rights reserved. No part of this publication may be reproduced, stored in a retrieval system, or transmitted in any form or by any means, electronic, mechanical, photocopying, recording, scanning, or otherwise, except as permitted under Section 107 or 108 of the 1976 United States Copyright Act, without either the prior written permission of the Publisher or authorization through payment of the appropriate per-copy fee to the Copyright Clearance Center, 222 Rosewood Drive, Danvers, MA 01923; (978) 750-8400; fax (978) 646-8600. Requests to the Publisher for permission should be addressed to the Permissions Department, c/o John Wiley & Sons, Inc., 111 River St., Hoboken, NJ 07030; (201) 748-8789, fax (201) 748-6326, www.wiley.com/go/permissions.

NEW DIRECTIONS FOR COMMUNITY COLLEGES (ISSN 0194-3081, electronic ISSN 1536-0733) is part of The Jossey-Bass Higher and Adult Education Series and is published quarterly by Wiley Subscription Services, Inc., A Wiley Company, at Jossey-Bass, One Montgomery St., Ste. 1200, San Francisco, CA 94104. Periodicals Postage Paid at San Francisco, California, and at additional mailing offices. POSTMASTER: Send address changes to New Directions for Community Colleges, Jossey-Bass, One Montgomery St., Ste. 1200, San Francisco, CA 94104.

SUBSCRIPTIONS cost $89 for individuals in the U.S., Canada, and Mexico, and $113 in the rest of the world for print only; $89 in all regions for electronic only; $98 in the U.S., Canada, and Mexico for combined print and electronic; $122 for combined print and electronic in the rest of the world. Institutional print only subscriptions are $292 in the U.S, $332 in Canada and Mexico, and $366 in the rest of the world; electronic only subscriptions are $292 in all regions; combined print and electronic subscriptions are $335 in the U.S. and $375 in Canada and Mexico.

EDITORIAL CORRESPONDENCE should be sent to the Editor-in-Chief, Arthur M. Cohen, at the Graduate School of Education and Information Studies, University of California, Box 951521, Los Angeles, CA 90095-1521. All manuscripts receive anonymous reviews by external referees.

New Directions for Community Colleges is indexed in CIJE: Current Index to Journals in Education (ERIC), Contents Pages in Education (T&F), Current Abstracts (EBSCO), Ed/Net (Simpson Communications), Education Index/Abstracts (H. W. Wilson), Educational Research Abstracts Online (T&F), ERIC Database (Education Resources Information Center), and Resources in Education (ERIC).

Microfilm copies of issues and articles are available in 16mm and 35mm, as well as microfiche in 105mm, through University Microfilms Inc., 300 North Zeeb Road, Ann Arbor, MI 48106-1346.

Contents

EDITORS' NOTES 1
Carrie B. Kisker, Richard L. Wagoner

1. Elements of Effective Transfer Associate Degrees 5
Carrie B. Kisker, Richard L. Wagoner, Arthur M. Cohen
This chapter outlines the elements of effective transfer associate degrees and discusses the policy impetuses of such reforms.

2. Transfer Associate Degrees in Historical Context 13
Arthur M. Cohen
The author examines transfer associate degrees from a historical perspective, arguing that their implementation moves America's system of higher education away from long-ingrained, isolated practices and toward greater trust and collaboration among institutions.

3. The Successful Transfer Structure in Washington State 17
Jane Sherman, Michelle Andreas
This chapter describes Washington State's effective and efficient transfer structure from historical and policy perspectives.

4. Widening and Wandering the Short Road to Success: The Louisiana Transfer Degree Guarantee 31
Kevin L. Cope
In this chapter, the author narrates the complex and often surprising process by which Louisiana deployed a transfer degree program in just two years.

5. Faculty-Determined Course Equivalency: The Key to Ohio's Transfer Mobility System 45
Paula K. Compton, Jonathan Tafel, Joe Law, Robert Gustafson
Ohio's process for developing a comprehensive, guaranteed transfer system that connects colleges and universities, high schools, adult career centers, and the workplace is detailed in this chapter.

6. Faculty Reflections on Implementing Associate Degrees for Transfer in California 55
Jane Patton, Michelle Pilati
This chapter describes California's intersegmental faculty-led system for implementing associate degrees for transfer.

7. The Role of Presidential Leadership in Improving New Jersey's Community College Transfer Experience 69
Casey Maliszewski, Kathleen Crabill, Lawrence Nespoli
Presidential leadership contributed to the implementation of New Jersey's transfer articulation legislation.

8. Developing a Culture of Transfer and Student Success in Arizona 79
Maria Harper-Marinick, Jeanne Swarthout
This chapter provides an overview of the transfer model in Arizona, as well as recent efforts to enhance collaborations among community colleges, universities, and public schools in the state.

9. Putting the Pieces Together and Asking the Hard Questions: Transfer Associate Degrees in Perspective 91
Richard L. Wagoner, Carrie B. Kisker
In this concluding chapter, the authors synthesize information from the volume, suggest a state-level model organizational structure for implementing transfer associate degrees, describe the interests and values of major constituencies in systemic transfer reforms, and note several hard questions that must be addressed if transfer associate degrees are to reach their full potential.

10. Sources and Information on Transfer Associate Degrees 105
Carlos Ayon
This annotated bibliography provides links to and short descriptions of statewide legislation authorizing or mandating the implementation of transfer associate degrees in several states, as well as scholarly articles and reports on the subject.

INDEX 111

Editors' Notes

In recent years, the federal government and several major philanthropic organizations have focused attention on the need to dramatically increase the number of bachelor's and other postsecondary degrees in order to retain the United States' economic competitiveness in a global marketplace. Improving what is often a complex and confusing community college-to-university transfer process, many analysts argue, is key to improving bachelor's degree production, as only a small proportion of community college students (25 to 35 percent, depending on the parameters used to define the likely transfer population) successfully move on to a four-year institution. And, as scholars have pointed out, even when students do transfer, some do so with a significant number of credits that do not apply toward a bachelor's degree, and many others make the transition without completing the full lower-division transfer curriculum or before earning an associate degree (Moore, Shulock, and Jensen, 2009). These patterns are costly, both to states and their students, and thus, over the past few years, several states have engaged in systemic transfer and articulation reforms, creating statewide pathways or degree programs that allow students to both earn an associate degree and transfer seamlessly into a state university with junior status.

Transfer associate degrees, as these pathways are often called, have been implemented in at least eight states, and several others are either in the process of developing them or are considering doing so. And although these degrees are relatively new to the education reform landscape, positive outcomes—in terms of both greater system efficiency and increased cost savings—have already been documented (Kisker, Wagoner, and Cohen, 2011). Indeed, transfer associate degrees have emerged as an effective way of significantly improving transfer and articulation, in the process increasing the number and percentage of bachelor's degree recipients within states and across the nation (Kisker, Cohen, and Wagoner, 2010).

A brief side note: Throughout the Editors' Notes to this volume, as well as Chapters One and Nine, we refer to these reforms as "transfer associate degrees," despite the fact that they may be known by different names in different parts of the country. Chapters Three through Eight, which are written by educators involved in the implementation of these degrees in various states, will utilize the specific terminology their state uses.

This volume of *New Directions for Community Colleges* emerged from research we conducted in 2010–2011 examining the implementation of transfer associate degrees in four states (Kisker, Wagoner, and Cohen, 2011). Through this work we found a significant amount of commonality in the processes used to implement the degrees, and identified seven curricular and policy-related elements of effective transfer associate degrees, four of which we believe are essential to the creation of significant statewide improvements in transfer and articulation. These effective elements of transfer associate degrees are described in detail in Chapter One, written by Carrie Kisker, Richard Wagoner, and Arthur Cohen. However, our investigation also led us to conclude that if transfer associate degrees are to reach their full potential, they must be implemented in ways that align with each state's unique history, policy goals, higher education capacity issues, and the academic cultures and traditions of its institutions.

This volume explores the implementation of transfer associate degrees from the perspectives of six states that have recently implemented all or some of the elements described in Chapter One. This state-by-state perspective provides the reader with an understanding of the various processes states have used to develop these degrees, as well as a sense of how educators in those states have worked to overcome unique and shared obstacles to degree implementation.

Following a brief sketch of how transfer associate degrees fit into the long history of efforts to improve community college-to-university transfer (Chapter Two, written by Arthur Cohen), the remainder of this volume is organized so that each chapter presents the process used to implement transfer associate degrees in a particular state while simultaneously highlighting a specific aspect important to the implementation process. In particular, Chapter Three, written by Jane Sherman and Michelle Andreas, outlines the successful structure built to support transfer in Washington State. The authors outline the major organizations responsible for developing and maintaining transfer policy, and take readers on a retrospective journey through the crucial events leading to the successful development and implementation of transfer associate degrees in that state. Chapter Four, written by Kevin Cope, provides a narrative account of the process of developing Louisiana's Transfer Degree Guarantee, and in particular its general education component. Punctuated with useful recommendations and astute observations of his state's fast-paced and often turbulent implementation process, this chapter will resonate with the many community college and university faculty members and administrators who have been (or will be) "dragged into" similar projects that require curriculum, policy, and articulation experts to venture out of their silos and work together toward a common goal.

Chapter Five, by Paula Compton, Jonathan Tafel, Joe Law, and Robert Gustafson, illustrates how Ohio has been able to balance faculty autonomy and system efficiency in the creation of transfer associate degrees through a system of faculty-determined course equivalency. The authors conclude by describing the hallmarks of Ohio's articulation and transfer system and by offering insights into why it has been successful. In Chapter Six, Jane Patton and Michelle Pilati further explore the importance of faculty-driven processes, describing how California's intersegmental, faculty-led system for developing transfer associate degrees both preserves local control of the curriculum and creates statewide transfer model curricula that can facilitate student movement among the state's 145 public colleges and universities.

Chapter Seven, written by Casey Maliszewski, Kathleen Crabill, and Lawrence Nespoli, draws upon the authors' recent experience implementing transfer associate degrees in New Jersey and explores the importance of presidential leadership in the process. The authors conclude with an analysis of how the state will continue to strengthen its transfer associate degrees and overall transfer process. Chapter Eight provides the final state-level perspective of transfer associate degrees, and demonstrates how Arizona's transfer infrastructure has evolved to incorporate K–12 educators. The authors, Maria Harper-Marinick and Jeanne Swarthout, describe the implementation of transfer associate degrees in that state, focusing on how Arizona has worked to develop a culture of transfer that extends beyond higher education's borders.

In Chapter Nine, Richard Wagoner and Carrie Kisker synthesize information from Chapters Three through Eight and suggest a state-level model organizational structure for implementing transfer associate degrees. They then discuss the interests and values of the major constituencies in systemic transfer reforms, and close by noting that despite the promise of these reforms, many of the hard questions related to transfer associate degrees—including their effectiveness in increasing transfer and baccalaureate completion over time—have yet to be answered. The volume concludes with a compendium of sources and information related to transfer associate degrees written by Carlos Ayon.

We hope that this volume of *New Directions for Community Colleges* will both celebrate the incredible progress many states have made toward improving the effectiveness and efficiency of the community college-to-university transfer process, as well as provide useful information about how transfer associate degrees have been implemented in some places and how they may be accomplished in others. We also hope that this volume will encourage states—both those who have already developed these degrees and those considering doing so—to rigorously assess the value add of these reforms over time. Evidence of success can be utilized in requests for additional legislative and monetary support, and indications that the degrees are not always working as expected can be used to modify and improve degree pathways to better serve students.

Carrie B. Kisker
Richard L. Wagoner
Editors

References

Kisker, C. B., Cohen, A. M., and Wagoner, R. L. *Reforming Transfer and Articulation in California: Four Statewide Solutions for Creating a More Successful and Seamless Transfer Path to the Baccalaureate.* Los Angeles: Center for the Study of Community Colleges, 2010.

Kisker, C. B., Wagoner, R. L., and Cohen, A. M. *Implementing Statewide Transfer and Articulation Reform: An Analysis of Transfer Associate Degrees in Four States.* Los Angeles: Center for the Study of Community Colleges, 2011.

Moore, C., Shulock, N., and Jensen, C. *Crafting a Student-Centered Transfer Process in California: Lessons from Other States.* Sacramento: California State University, Sacramento, Institute for Higher Education Leadership and Policy, 2009.

CARRIE B. KISKER is an education research and policy consultant in Los Angeles, California, as well as a director of the Center for the Study of Community Colleges.

RICHARD L. WAGONER is assistant professor of higher education at the University of California, Los Angeles, and a director of the Center for the Study of Community Colleges.

This chapter discusses the policy impetuses behind statewide pathways that simultaneously lead to an associate degree and transfer with junior status to a four-year college or university, then outlines the elements of effective transfer associate degrees.

Elements of Effective Transfer Associate Degrees

Carrie B. Kisker, Richard L. Wagoner, Arthur M. Cohen

In recent years, a convergence of several forces—increased legislative involvement in higher education, governmental and philanthropic pressure to increase postsecondary degree and certificate production, demands for a highly trained workforce, and fiscal belt-tightening at colleges and universities across America—has resulted in efforts to significantly reform community college-to-university transfer and articulation processes. One increasingly popular method of reform is the implementation of transfer associate degrees: statewide pathways or degree programs that allow students to both earn an associate degree from a community college and transfer seamlessly into a state university with junior status. (*Note:* These degrees are known by different names in different states, but for the purposes of clarity, we refer to all of them as transfer associate degrees.)

The reasons for implementing transfer associate degrees are myriad. From an efficiency standpoint, states view these transfer pathways as vehicles for aligning lower-division general education and premajor curricula across two- and four-year institutions, thereby reducing course overlap and the need to repeat similar courses after transferring. In addition, there is emerging evidence that transfer associate degrees better prepare community college students for upper-division work, and that students transferring with such degrees are more likely to persist at a university, complete a greater number of credit hours, and pass more courses (Hezel Associates, 2007; Kisker, Wagoner, and Cohen, 2011; Mustafa, Glenn, and Compton, 2010). Furthermore, recent data show that transfer associate degrees in

Arizona and Washington have resulted in significant reductions in the amount of time and number of credits earned en route to a bachelor's degree (Hezel Associates, 2007; Stern, Pitman, and Pavelchek, 2009).

These efficiency gains, many argue, lead directly to cost savings for both states and students. And indeed, a recent report from the Ohio Board of Regents indicates that the state's transfer reform activities save $20 million annually, and that roughly one-third of those cost savings are attributable to transfer associate degrees (Mustafa, Glenn, and Compton, 2010). Furthermore, the gains in efficiency allow for more students to enter and succeed in public postsecondary systems. As California's Campaign for College Opportunity (2012) recently reported, the implementation of that state's landmark transfer associate degree legislation has made it possible for 53,000 additional students to be served in the California Community Colleges and California State University systems.

Transfer associate degrees are also desirable from a student's standpoint. They provide recipients with greater flexibility and more options in transfer, as these degrees are based on general education packages and lower-division major pathways that are common across a state's community colleges and public universities. Students earning transfer associate degrees are assured that their credits will transfer and apply at multiple institutions—a benefit that is especially important for those students who are more interested in transferring to a specific degree program than to a particular university. Greater flexibility for transfer students also benefits states experiencing enrollment constraints within certain institutions or degree programs.

Finally, transfer associate degrees are viewed by lawmakers and system leaders as key to increasing the number of community college-to-university transfers, as well as boosting the number of bachelor's and other postsecondary degrees awarded annually. This outcome fits nicely within the completion agenda set by the Obama administration and pushed in large part by several major philanthropic organizations. Although most of the states that have implemented transfer associate degrees have done so relatively recently, reports from Washington and Ohio show that transfer associate degrees have had a positive effect on transfer rates, and that the implementation of these degrees has spurred greater degree completion at both the associate and bachelor's degree levels (Mustafa, Glenn, and Compton, 2010; Stern, Pitman, and Pavelchek, 2009; Washington Higher Education Coordinating Board, 2006).

Of course, transfer associate degrees are not a panacea, and the individual and institutional challenges that have kept transfer rates hovering around 25 percent nationally for the past 30 years (Szelenyi, 2002) will not be eliminated by this reform strategy. Indeed, some argue that these degrees and similar reforms to statewide articulation policies are more likely to facilitate the transfer process by preventing the loss of credits and improving time to degree than they are to improve the number or percentage of students who transfer. As Roska and Keith (2008) argue, the main purpose of articulation reforms "is to ease the process for students who have *already* decided to transfer," not to encourage more students to do so (p. 237, emphasis in the original). Furthermore, transfer associate degrees are far from easy to implement (as later chapters in this volume will attest), and are not always supported by faculty who may resist what they see as an encroachment on their academic freedom and curricular autonomy. Transfer and articulation officers, advisors, and registrars also may resist the implementation of transfer associate degrees, as these pathways fundamentally change the way that community college students should be advised and often run counter to long-standing local priority and other articulation arrangements. Despite these challenges, transfer associate degrees have been or are being implemented in many states, including Arizona, California, Florida, Louisiana, New Jersey, North Carolina, Ohio, Oregon, South Carolina, and Washington. Other states—Texas, for example—have created some but not all components of the degrees.

This chapter draws from a report we published in April 2011 titled "Implementing Statewide Transfer & Articulation Reform: An Analysis of Transfer Associate Degrees in Four States" (Kisker, Wagoner, and Cohen, 2011). The purpose of that project—which was generously funded by the Bill & Melinda Gates and Walter S. Johnson Foundations—was to examine the political processes, actors, and associations involved in systemic transfer and articulation reforms in four states (Arizona, New Jersey, Ohio, and Washington) in order to describe implementation strategies that may be successfully utilized in states that are currently embarking on or planning for similar reforms. Our analysis of the elements of effective transfer associate degrees, presented in the following pages, emerged from site visits, examination of relevant documents, and roughly 60 in-depth qualitative interviews with policymakers, system leaders, college presidents and key administrators, faculty, and others involved in implementing transfer associate degrees in the four states under review.

Elements of Effective Transfer Associate Degrees

Transfer associate degrees can be understood as a grouping of seven curricular and policy-related elements: (1) a common general education (GE) package; (2) common lower-division premajor and early-major pathways; (3) a focus on credit applicability; (4) junior status upon transfer; (5) guaranteed and/or priority university admission; (6) associate and/or bachelor's degree credit limits; and (7) an acceptance policy for upper-division courses. The first four elements, with one exception, were implemented in all four states included in our 2011 study, and we believe that they are essential to the creation of significant statewide improvements in transfer and articulation. The final three elements are also important but may be more or less necessary, depending on each state's unique history, policy goals, capacity issues, and the academic cultures and traditions of its institutions.

A Common General Education Pattern. All four of the states included in our 2011 analysis and several others throughout the nation, including Louisiana (whose transfer associate degrees are discussed further in Chapter Four), have created general education (GE) packages or modules that are common across the state's community colleges, and that transfer en bloc to the public universities. These GE packages are accepted in lieu of the receiving institution's own GE pattern, providing students with a set of GE classes that is portable anywhere in the state. A common GE package is the foundation upon which transfer associate degrees are built, and is key to achieving statewide gains in efficiency and cost savings.

Common Lower-Division Premajor and Early-Major Pathways. Although New Jersey has yet to incorporate common lower-division premajor and early-major pathways into its statewide transfer policy, Arizona, Ohio, and Washington have all developed these sequences in various disciplines, and California has done so for at least 25 majors. Because common lower-division major pathways are guaranteed to apply toward the major at receiving universities, they are widely viewed as key to reducing excess credits and improving time-to-degree among transfer students. They also provide students with greater flexibility to transfer anywhere in the state within their program of study; this is especially important in popular or overenrolled programs. Ohio has developed a process for determining course equivalency based on adherence to specified learning outcomes that has allowed that state to develop pre- or early-major pathways in 40 academic disciplines, as well as 17 career-technical areas. Ohio's approach is discussed in more detail in Chapter Five.

A Focus on Credit Applicability. For transfer associate degrees to be successful in improving system efficiency, achieving cost savings, and creating greater flexibility and options for transfer students, policymakers and educators implementing the degrees must move beyond consideration of course transferability and focus instead on how credits will apply to specific academic and degree requirements at receiving institutions. This is especially important when developing those courses or sequences that will apply toward a student's major. Ideally, two- and four-year faculty can work together to agree upon common lower-division pathways that can transfer and apply seamlessly at all public universities in a state. In practice, however, enacting common lower-division sequences, especially in the major, can run counter to long-held traditions of institutional autonomy and academic freedom. While the latter does not preclude the former, honoring the values of autonomy and freedom, as well as those of efficiency, student centeredness, and the common good, requires a delicate balancing act.

Junior Status upon Transfer. The assumption that transfer associate degrees will apply toward a student's program of study at receiving universities leads directly to the requirement, in place in all four states we examined, that students transferring with these degrees be automatically granted junior status, with all of the rights and privileges such status typically entails (for example, priority registration over lower-division students). Furthermore, these students should be considered for scholarships and/or acceptance into specific degree programs on the same basis as native university students. Automatic conferral of junior status upon transfer leads to greater efficiency and cost savings by incenting students to complete the full lower-division curriculum at a community college and by helping to ensure that—barring changes in major—students can complete a baccalaureate in the standard amount of time and credits.

Guaranteed and/or Priority University Admission. Guaranteed and/or priority university admission for students with transfer associate degrees removes incentives for students to transfer prior to earning an associate degree (which is, from a state policy perspective, a less efficient transfer pattern), and instead rewards degree completion. Furthermore, such policies ensure that students are well prepared for upper-division study in their major. Most states with a guaranteed admissions policy—Arizona, Ohio, and Washington, for example—certify that transfer associate degree holders with at least a 2.0 grade point average will be granted admission somewhere within the state, but not necessarily to any particular university or degree program, allowing institutions to set their own admissions standards. Transfer associate degree recipients in Ohio also receive priority admission over out-of-state associate degree graduates and transfer students, and Washington gives students with transfer associate degrees priority consideration over nondegreed transfers.

Associate and/or Bachelor's Degree Credit Limits. Many states with transfer associate degrees have instituted limits on the number of units that can be counted toward a transfer associate degree, and several also limit the number of credits in a bachelor's degree. For example, New Jersey's Comprehensive State-Wide Transfer Agreement states that transfer associate degree recipients will have completed exactly half of the units required for a bachelor's degree, and that universities must graduate transfer students within the same number of upper-division units. Similarly, transfer associate degrees in Arizona can include one-half of bachelor's degree requirements (typically 120 semester credits) plus one course, and in California, the state universities are prohibited from requiring transfer students to take more than 60 units to complete a 120-unit bachelor's degree. These credit-limit policies help to reduce course overlap and improve time-to-degree among transfer students.

Acceptance Policy for Upper-Division Courses. Some states have also written policies regarding the transferability and applicability of upper-division coursework into their statewide transfer policies, although the intent of these policies varies widely among the four states we examined for our 2011 report. For example, the Ohio Articulation and Transfer Policy (Ohio Board of Regents, 2010) affirms that if a course completed as part of the lower-division curriculum at the sending institution (typically a community college) is deemed equivalent to an upper-division course at the receiving institution, it will be counted as upper-division credit. By contrast, New Jersey's policy states that, "by definition, 300- and 400-level courses at four-year institutions have no course equivalents at the community colleges" (New Jersey Presidents' Council, 2008).

Policies regarding the acceptance of upper-division courses may help to reduce course overlap, improve time- and credits-to-degree among transfer students, and improve system efficiency, but unless they are implemented cautiously, with significant input and guidance from disciplinary faculty, they may go too far toward standardizing degree requirements, and in the process reduce institutions' ability to provide unique and cutting-edge academic programs. Nonetheless, these policies may be especially useful and even necessary in states struggling with university capacity issues and/or those where a significant number of students do not live in geographic proximity to a four-year university.

While we believe that transfer associate degrees should contain all or many of the elements described in the preceding paragraphs if they are to be most effective in accomplishing the statewide policy objectives of greater system efficiency, improved flexibility and options for students, increased transfer and degree completion, and cost savings for students and states, there is much room for these elements to be interpreted and implemented in ways that support each state's unique history, policy goals, and academic cultures and traditions. Chapters Three through Eight in this volume further explore the ways in which elements of transfer associate degrees have been put into practice in various states across the nation. In addition, systemic transfer reforms will not be a panacea for all the challenges community college students face in preparing for and succeeding after transfer. Transfer associate degrees must be coupled with continued support for students, who often know very little about transfer pathways, proper course sequences, and expectations for college-level work. As additional states implement transfer associate degrees, and as the results of these reforms are evaluated over time, we will have stronger evidence with which to judge how effectively these degrees meet their stated policy objectives, and more information to share about how various elements of the degrees may be adopted or adapted in other regions or at other points in the education pipeline.

References

Campaign for College Opportunity. "Historic Community College Transfer Legislation—16 Months Later." *Campaign for College Opportunity Newsletter*, 2012, 8(2).

Hezel Associates. *Evaluation of Arizona's Transfer Articulation System*. Syracuse, N.Y.: Hezel Associates, 2007. Retrieved Mar. 15, 2012, from www.hezelassociates.com/resources/46-evaluation-of-arizonas-transfer-articulation-system.

Kisker, C. B., Wagoner, R. L., and Cohen, A. M. *Implementing Statewide Transfer & Articulation Reform: An Analysis of Transfer Associate Degrees in Four States.* Los Angeles: Center for the Study of Community Colleges, 2011. Retrieved Mar. 15, 2012, from http://centerforcommunitycolleges.org/index.php/projects-and-publications/current-projects/.

Mustafa, S., Glenn, D., and Compton, P. *Transfers in the University System of Ohio: State Initiatives and Outcomes 2002–2009.* Columbus: Ohio Board of Regents, 2010. Retrieved Mar. 15, 2012, from http://regents.ohio.gov/transfer/research/transfer-students-in-uso.pdf.

New Jersey Presidents' Council. *Comprehensive State-wide Transfer Agreement.* Trenton, N.J.: New Jersey Presidents' Council, 2008. Retrieved Mar. 15, 2012, from www.nj.gov/highereducation/PDFs/XferAgreementOct08.pdf.

Ohio Board of Regents. *Ohio Transfer and Articulation Policy.* Columbus: Ohio Board of Regents, 2010. Retrieved Mar. 15, 2012, from http://regents.ohio.gov/transfer/policy/CreditTransferPolicy.pdf.

Roska, J., and Keith, B. "Credits, Time, and Attainment: Articulation Policies and Success after Transfer." *Educational Evaluation and Policy Analysis,* 2008, *30*(3), 236–254.

Stern, P., Pitman, K., and Pavelchek, D. *The Role of Transfer in the Attainment of Bachelor's Degrees at Washington Public Baccalaureate Institutions, Class of 2006.* Olympia: Washington State University, Social & Economic Sciences Research Center, Puget Sound Division, 2009. Retrieved Mar. 15, 2012, from www.hecb.wa.gov/sites/default/files/HECB%20Transfer%20Study%20FINAL.pdf.

Szelenyi, K. *National Transfer Rates Are Up! Results of the 2001 Transfer Assembly Project.* Los Angeles: Center for the Study of Community Colleges, 2002. (ED 482 719)

Washington Higher Education Coordinating Board. *Consolidated Transfer Report: Transfer Policy and Upper-Division Baccalaureate Capacity.* Olympia: Washington Higher Education Coordinating Board, 2006. (ED 498 217)

CARRIE B. KISKER is an education research and policy consultant in Los Angeles, California, as well as a director of the Center for the Study of Community Colleges.

RICHARD L. WAGONER is assistant professor of higher education at the University of California, Los Angeles, and a director of the Center for the Study of Community Colleges.

ARTHUR M. COHEN is emeritus professor of higher education at the University of California, Los Angeles, and founder of the Center for the Study of Community Colleges.

2

The implementation of transfer associate degrees moves America's system of higher education away from long-ingrained, isolated practices and toward greater trust and collaboration among institutions.

Transfer Associate Degrees in Historical Context

Arthur M. Cohen

When public junior colleges entered the American educational scene early in the twentieth century, their first and still major function was to serve as a gateway to the baccalaureate. The earliest college in California received state authorization for course reimbursement by arguing that Fresno was 200 miles from Berkeley, thus penalizing young people from California's central valley who sought bachelor's degrees. At around the same time the University of Chicago began accrediting the courses offered by Joliet Junior College.

High school expansion allowed the universities that were striving to become Germanic-style research and professional development centers to reduce the basic education that occupied a substantial portion of their curriculum, but many young people who sought entry still fell short of university expectations for literacy and general education. The universities expected junior colleges to fill that gap by teaching basic studies to freshmen and sophomores, whereupon those students could transfer to their upper division.

But almost as soon as public junior colleges had been established their leaders began agitating to add vocational education, programs that did not match those offered by universities. In the 1920s around 25 percent of the community college curriculum was occupationally related. Even though it took half a century before enrollment in vocational studies reached parity with those in general education and the liberal arts, those programs limited the proportion of two-year college students who went on to baccalaureate-granting institutions.

Two-year college involvement with community services and adult education, especially adult literacy, resulted in further limitations as most participants in these programs were not interested in degrees. A preponderance of remedial studies also restricted transfer. And the students attending part-time, which for decades has accounted for around 60 percent of total enrollment, have always transferred at lower rates than the full-timers.

Transfer education centering on the liberal arts declined relatively beginning in the late 1960s with the expansion of vocational education. But the distinctions blurred as courses that matched university programs in business and health fields grew. By the 1970s more than half all associate degrees awarded were to students from occupational programs, and one third of all transfers had occupationally oriented majors.

The ratio of bachelor's degrees awarded to students who began their postsecondary studies in community colleges has never approximated those granted to native university freshmen. However, when viewed from the other end of the spectrum—that is, when one counts the number and percent of bachelor's degree recipients who earned credits from a community college—the transfer picture takes different form. According to a National Student Clearinghouse study of 3,000 institutions, 45 percent of students obtaining bachelor's degrees in 2010–2011 had community college credits on their transcripts. Of these, 24 percent had spent 1 term in community college; 16 percent, 2 terms; 19 percent, 3 or 4 terms; 15 percent, 5 or 6 terms; 14 percent, 7 to 9 terms; and 12 percent, 10 or more terms. The states with the highest number of transfers were California, New York, Texas, Arizona, and Pennsylvania. Those with the highest percentage of transfers completing bachelor's degrees were Texas, Wyoming, California, Kansas, and Oregon (National Student Clearinghouse, 2012).

Over the past few decades, many efforts have been made to increase the number of bachelor's degrees awarded to community college matriculants. Chief among these are articulation agreements, which have attempted to have the universities accept general education courses at full value, as well as common course numbering and curriculum guides. But the universities have always had the greater say in controlling the transfer process: specifying the types of courses accepted; accepting students to particular majors; evaluating the credits to be counted toward degree requirements; and setting prerequisites for various majors.

Perhaps as a result, the past 20 years have seen the initiation and growth of community colleges offering their own bachelor's degrees. Now at least 15 states authorize the community college baccalaureate, although to date these have been restricted to occupationally related programs, chiefly teacher education and business and health fields. Some of these colleges have been newly designated as four-year institutions and the Carnegie Classification System has opened a category, "Baccalaureate

Associate Colleges," to account for institutions offering at least 10 percent of their degrees at the bachelor's level.

The transfer associate degree described in this volume is another recent development, one that attempts to improve the efficiency and effectiveness of the transfer process through statewide articulation agreements and policies that limit individual universities' ability to impose additional requirements on students. No state or system has solved the overriding problem, however: ensuring that specific credits earned at community colleges satisfy all general education requirements for the baccalaureate and serve as prerequisites for all majors. Yet many states have taken steps closer to this scenario by implementing transfer associate degrees. The implementation of these degrees has not been immune from long-held views of institutional autonomy and faculty academic freedom, but they have nonetheless remained politically expedient, as the proportion of low-income students and students of color is higher at community colleges, and because the cost of education is lower.

From a broader historical perspective, the practice of implementing systemic transfer and articulation reform in which a number of states are engaged is no small task. It is an exercise in modifying the course of higher education away from the culture it has developed over a century or more. With the legislation and implementation of transfer associate degrees, states are moving away from the following:

- The closed classroom door, where the individual faculty member, occasionally acting with other professors but only within a disciplinary department, is the sole arbiter of the curriculum.
- Separate institutions setting the criteria for student entry and progress toward degrees of their own design.
- Staff members unaware of what their colleagues are doing (i.e., the counselors, institutional researchers, faculty, and administrators all acting as though their activities are unrelated to anything outside their offices).
- Research productivity (for universities) and the number of students exposed to classroom teaching (for community colleges) as the dominant criteria of institutional worth.
- Student hours spent in proximity to instructors as measures of learning achieved.

The shift is occurring in four main directions. The first is toward competency-based learning outcomes. This reform has been posited for a half century at least, but higher education's inertia has retarded it. Few faculty in any sector have been trained in the specification and use of measurable objectives, which demands holding the course goals constant and modifying the media as necessary to bring the group to the predetermined achievement level (Bloom, 1968). Most are too ready to fall back on the argument that a variety of student types precludes such advance determination.

The second direction is toward system-wide lower-division curriculum design under legislative oversight, and it is not occurring without hitting major stumbling blocks. Throughout the history of higher education in America, each department within each college has controlled most aspects of course design. Getting the numerous collectivities to accept external controls has not been impossible, but is a daunting task, especially when outsiders such as state-level legislators are involved.

With the implementation of transfer associate degrees states are also moving toward greater inter-institutional cooperation and trust. Most colleges began and have developed as independent entities. The staff in one rarely knows or interacts with the staff in another, even when they are in the same district. As such, building trust across institutional and departmental boundaries remains a foreign element, yet it is essential for successful implementation of common college outcomes.

Finally, the implementation of transfer associate degrees and other statewide transfer reforms has highlighted the need for a sizeable percentage of faculty, counselors, and administrators at all types of institutions to be knowledgeable about and concerned with student progress. Further, for a system to succeed in producing verifiable learning, professionals at all levels must be committed to the forms of assessment necessary in maintaining it. This requires a big step toward cooperation because the colleges are not, and will not, be managed by autocrats.

It's a big order ... make it happen.

References

Bloom, B. *Learning for Mastery* (Evaluation Comment 1). Los Angeles: University of California, Los Angeles, Center for the Study of Evaluation, 1968.

National Student Clearinghouse. *The Role of Two-Year Institutions in Four-Year Success.* Herndon, Va.: Author, 2012. Retrieved Sept. 17, 2012, from www.studentclearinghouse.info/snapshot/docs/SnapshotReport6-TwoYearContributions.pdf.

ARTHUR M. COHEN is emeritus professor of higher education at the University of California, Los Angeles, and founder of the Center for the Study of Community Colleges.

3

This chapter describes the structure of transfer in Washington State within a historical and policy context. The focus is on how and why the state's transfer system is effective for institutions and efficient for students.

The Successful Transfer Structure in Washington State

Jane Sherman, Michelle Andreas

How did Washington create a clear organizational structure that assigns responsibility for each aspect of transfer policy to the group that is best suited to manage it (Kisker, Wagoner, and Cohen, 2011)? In this chapter we will introduce the agencies, organizations, and entities that have played a key role in gathering information, analyzing data, negotiating interests, and implementing transfer policy in Washington State. We also describe the critical events that shaped Washington's successful 40-year history of transferring students from community and technical colleges to independent and public universities, as well as more recent policies that will shape our future. We end the chapter with a quick summary of some secrets to our state's transfer system success.

The Major Players in Washington's Transfer Structure

An organizational structure involving committed decision-makers with position authority at the state's independent and public higher education institutions is critical to Washington's transfer success. Two groups now fill this role. The Joint Transfer Council (formerly the Joint Access Oversight Group) was created to oversee major policy issues related to transfer. The Intercollege Relations Committee (ICRC) provides an important communication venue and monitors compliance with state transfer agreements.

The Joint Transfer Council. Anchoring Washington's transfer structure is the Joint Transfer Council (JTC), which was formed in 2005. The

JTC evaluates statewide transfer issues, commissions the development of new transfer degrees, and recommends policy strategies and solutions to all sectors of higher education. It is a standing committee that meets four times a year. The JTC is composed of the vice provost for academic affairs (or similar titles, for example, dean of undergraduate education) from each of the six public baccalaureate institutions, two registration or academic planning officers from independent, nonprofit baccalaureate institutions, and eight vice presidents of instruction or student services at community and technical colleges.

Key to the success of the JTC is the equal representation between two-year and four-year sectors, plus the commitment to operate by consensus rather than by voting. The initial decision to operate by consensus was a trust-building strategy by the group, which came into being at a relatively low point in the cycle of intersector relationships. The original membership realized—and the current membership affirms—that while the group might not be able to sustain unanimity on every issue in the future, a 40-year history of statewide, mutually agreed upon, transfer agreements is a strong incentive to work hard to maintain a consensus-based structure.

Membership in the JTC has been long-term for most representatives, with slow turnover allowing new members the opportunity to readily absorb the group culture of trust, commitment, flexibility, and thoughtful deliberation. The JTC is supported by staff from the Washington Student Achievement Council (WSAC, formerly the Higher Education Coordinating Board or HECB), the State Board for Community and Technical Colleges (SBCTC), the Council of Presidents (COP) representing public universities, and Independent Colleges of Washington (ICW). WSAC provides strategic planning, oversight, and advocacy for Washington's higher education system. SBCTC provides leadership and coordination for Washington's 34 public community and technical colleges. COP is a voluntary association whose leadership is comprised of the presidents of the six public baccalaureate degree granting college and universities. ICW is an association of 10 private, nonprofit colleges in the state. The JTC works on behalf of the institutions and sectors represented by the membership, in collaboration with other entities concerned with transfer, especially the Intercollege Relations Commission.

The greatest challenge for the JTC is that final approval of systemic change takes time. All constituent groups must have input, and each sector has its own approval process. The members of the JTC report to and take direction from their own institutions and sectors—the JTC does not, itself, report to any other entity. The normal length of time for full approval of a policy change is approximately one year. In addition, assessing the effectiveness of actions affecting a large system over time is difficult, so it can be challenging to evaluate the value added by the JTC on any individual issue.

The Intercollege Relations Commission. The ICRC, organized under the constitution of the Washington Council on High School–College

Relations (WCHSCR) in 1970, is the *grande dame* of transfer in Washington. Over 40 years ago, this group worked out the state's original transfer agreement, which not only specified the requirements for the degree but ensured that its recipients would be able to transfer and apply all lower-division, general education credits at all public and most private four-year colleges and universities.

The ICRC is comprised of representatives appointed by the presidents of 30 community and technical college districts, 6 public baccalaureate institutions, 10 independent non-profit institutions and, most recently, Western Governor's University-Washington. There are at least 50 members in attendance at the semiannual meetings, with numbers heavily weighted toward community and technical colleges. Like the JTC, the ICRC is supported by staff members from the WSAC, SBCTC, COP, and ICW.

According to their Handbook (WCHSCR, 2009, p. 16), which is the bible for transfer in Washington, the role of the ICRC is to "facilitate the transfer of students and credits between and among community colleges and baccalaureate institutions; to provide continuous evaluation and review of transfer degrees, programs, policies, procedures, and inter-institutional relationships ... ; to provide ways to resolve disputes regarding degrees, course equivalencies, and other transfer-related problems ... ; and to promote articulation among the programs and curricula of member institutions." During recent years, the ICRC has focused on improving and monitoring the transfer process. This effort involves reviewing compliance with the guidelines at the colleges, surfacing issues that may require systemic solutions, and communicating relevant information about programs, schools, and students. Several schools per year are visited by the ICRC Transfer Review Committee, which produces a confidential report to help schools improve their student transfer procedures and prevents drift that could endanger the statewide agreements. The JTC and ICRC work closely together, including requesting assistance from each other on matters within each group's purview. The JTC has recently made two recommendations to ICRC: that they include the public and independent colleges and universities in their reviews, and that all reviews be made public to stakeholders.

Higher Education Sector Groups. Each higher education sector has decision-making bodies that operate broadly, but that include acting on recommendations from its sector's JTC representatives among its responsibilities. Community and technical college transfer policies are vetted through the Washington Association of Community and Technical Colleges (WACTC), which is the organization of community and technical college presidents. The WACTC structure includes, among others, the Instruction Commission, which is comprised of vice presidents of instruction at each community and technical college. The Instruction Commission has primary responsibility for recommending transfer policy to the

WACTC, and individuals from the Instruction Commission also serve on the JTC.

The public baccalaureate provosts meet as the Interinstitutional Committee of Academic Officers (ICAO), a subgroup of the Council of Presidents. Issues relating to transfer are raised and/or reviewed within this group, and recommendations of the JTC acted upon.

The independent baccalaureate institutions meet through the Independent Colleges of Washington (ICW). In general, the 10 ICW institutions attempt to be as consistent as possible with the publics, and their representatives are integral partners in the Joint Transfer Council. However, their more varied missions and perspectives do lead, at times, to some variation such as required courses in religion and philosophy.

JTC members from each of these groups make recommendations to their respective academic policymaking bodies and obtain their approval, after which the JTC formally approves any policy change and specifies its implementation date.

40 Years of Direct Transfer in Washington State

Washington's transfer structure developed gradually, over time, with each step and each new entity a specific response to an identified gap in the ability of the system to respond effectively to a systemic transfer challenge. The following discussion of the evolution of the transfer structure will highlight the important components of Washington's transfer process as it was developed.

Washington's first junior college was started in 1915 in Everett when 42 students began a one-year college program on the top floor of Everett High School. By 1941 eight junior colleges operated in Washington with combined enrollment of approximately 1,000. In 1961, junior colleges in the state were designated as "community" colleges, and in 1967 were recognized by the Washington State Legislature in the Community College Act. In 1991, the state's five public vocational technical institutions, formerly under the jurisdiction of local school districts, were designated as "technical colleges," and merged with the community college system (SBCTC, 2012).

Crucial Event 1: Growing Numbers of Transfer Students, Can We Get Together? The growth in community colleges in the early 1960s brought with it a significant number of students who were transferring courses and credits from community colleges to four-year colleges and universities. The need for improved communication and coordination among higher education institutions became pressing. In 1968, the WCHSCR established a junior-senior college committee, which began ongoing communications to smooth the transition for transfer students.

In 1970 the Washington Association of Community College Presidents and the presidents of public and private baccalaureate institutions agreed on a structural model for addressing transfer and articulation in the state. The ICRC was thus organized under the constitution of the WCHSCR. The ICRC also developed a constitution, sponsored transfer advisor workshops, focused on problems related to transfer of credit, and established an institutional hotline.

When the first transfer associate degree guidelines were developed by the ICRC in 1971, all institutions of higher education in the state subscribed to a single transfer degree, with similar characteristics, rather than unique degrees from each institution. Awkwardly saddled ever since with the name of the agreement rather than that of the degree, the direct transfer agreement degree is often characterized as simply "the DTA." The core of the agreement is that a 90-quarter-credit associate degree, which includes the agreed-upon number of credits in each of the traditional areas of knowledge (English/communication, quantitative reasoning, humanities, science, social sciences), will transfer intact, will complete the lower-division general education requirements at the receiving institution, and may include up to 15 credits of otherwise nontransferable (technical/vocational) coursework. Students are incented to complete the degree prior to transfer, as without it, they are required to meet all of the general education requirements of the receiving institution. Institutions vary both in their general education patterns and in the courses that fit into each curricular "bucket." Indeed, some institutions require courses quite similar to their own, while others are more liberal in their interpretation of acceptable courses for non-DTA transfer students.

The existence of these early collaborative efforts and the agreements they engendered have been a key to the willingness among all sectors to continue working to improve transfer (WCHSCR, 2009, pp. 3, 4).

Crucial Event 2: The Legislature Threatens—Can We Do It on Our Own? In the early 1980s, in the face of inconsistencies both among and within institutions in the implementation of the DTA, the legislature threatened to intervene. Some institutions were known or believed to be "discounting" grades (transferring in a lower GPA than was actually earned at the community college), filling selective programs with their own students before transfer students had a chance to apply, or otherwise disadvantaging transfer students, though with all good intentions of providing adequately for their freshman-entry students. In response to institutional and student complaints—not to mention unspecified Legislative threats to "fix" transfer—ICRC developed an agreement known as the Umbrella Policy (WCHSCR, 2009, pp. 15–17). This policy covers a number of topics that ensured parity in treatment between transfer and freshman-entry students in terms of courses, credits, and grades, and affirmed that the award of the direct transfer agreement degree generally included completion of general education requirements at any of the four-year schools. For the first time, the WSAC approved an agreement as official policy, which gave the agreement added weight. *With the Umbrella Policy, institutions of higher education* and the legislature both gained confidence in the efficacy of collaboration and negotiation.

Crucial Event 3: Will Transfer Students Have a Place to Transfer To? In 1994, community and technical college presidents became alarmed that more and more of their transfer students would not have a seat at public baccalaureate institutions due to increasing numbers of graduating high school seniors. Public baccalaureate institutions, however, were heavily recruiting high school graduates to provide sufficient numbers of lower-division students to ensure institutional financial stability.

In response to this quandary, an intersector transfer task force facilitated by the WSAC wrestled long and hard to reach what became known as the Proportionality Agreement. The agreement states that each public baccalaureate institution will maintain its 1992 proportion of community college transfer student enrollments in relation to entering freshman enrollments, with priority given to students who have obtained an associate degree or cannot otherwise progress, meaning they have reached the limit of 90 transferable credits (WSAC, 1994).

The Proportionality Agreement was intended to ensure that all resident transfer students who have completed the DTA have an opportunity to transfer to a public university. *The WSAC's role in adopting as policy the agreement reached among institutions and sectors provided the official imprimatur that has kept it in force.*

Crucial Event 4: How Do We Best Prepare STEM Transfer Students? In the late 1990s, students, employers, and legislators were placing new pressure on institutions of higher education to produce more science, technology, engineering, and math (STEM) graduates. A review of data by the SBCTC and COP revealed that students who transferred from community colleges into STEM majors at baccalaureate institutions were accumulating far more credits upon graduation than freshman-entry students at those institutions.

Again, the sectors came together to devise a solution: a science transfer degree that would allow community college students to take sufficient science and math premajor courses prior to transfer without sacrificing their general education completion advantage. By eliminating all free elective credits and dropping 15 humanities/social science credits, all of the needed math and science courses could be included in a 90-credit associate degree. But there was a snag: Electives could be picked up later, but what about those 15 general education credits? Ultimately, the baccalaureate institutions agreed to accept the associate of science transfer (AS-T) degree as if it were a DTA, and to require only the missing 15 humanities/social sciences credits for completion of general education requirements (as opposed to the receiving institution's entire pattern of general education coursework). Thus, in 2000, Washington's higher education sectors adopted two tracks of the AS-T (one for the biological, environmental, and earth sciences, as well as chemistry and geology, and one for engineering and computer sciences) to assist transfer students who seek entry into competitive programs in the sciences. Both AS-Ts provide students with completion of lower-division general education requirements similar to first- and second-year university students in engineering and other science-based fields, as well as priority admission over other transfer students at most public university science and engineering programs. *Quantitative evidence was an important impetus for policy development, and its use was reinforced by the subsequent data showing that students transferring with the AS-T degrees were more efficiently completing bachelor's degrees than students who had transferred with only a DTA or without a degree* (SBCTC, 2012).

Crucial Event 5: How Can We Maintain Current Agreements? In the early 2000s, it became apparent to higher education decision makers that, while the ICRC had engendered a superb DTA, it would not be able to successfully maneuver through the shoals of evolving curricula. Over the years, membership in the ICRC had moved from vice provosts and instructional vice presidents to directors of admissions at baccalaureate institutions and deans of instruction at community and technical colleges. In addition, the ICRC included 30 community and technical college representatives, far outnumbering the public and independent baccalaureate representatives on the commission. It was inevitable that any issue that divided the group by sector would eventually grind to a halt.

In 2005, the issue of who should approve new academic electives for inclusion in the DTA became a pivotal issue, as it had festered unresolved for several years and was beginning to poison important relationships. As a result, a "rogue" group of long-time, multisector colleagues gathered several times over a kitchen table to jump-start a solution. The JTC evolved out of these "secret" conversations among colleagues who were convinced that the deliberations of the ICRC could provide the foundation for more efficient and substantive changes in the system, *if the conversations could be elevated to a higher level at the baccalaureate institutions, if the numbers could be equalized, and if trust could be rebuilt among all the higher education representatives.*

The new JTC's solution to the long-simmering problem of who could approve the inclusion of new academic electives in the DTA degree is a good case of "cutting through a Gordian knot." The JTC recommendation was simply to authorize the SBCTC to approve new academic electives, but with the option that the baccalaureates could challenge specific additions through the JTC, which to date has never happened.

After its establishment in 2005, the JTC took on the task of revising the original DTA. Substantive changes to this seminal agreement had not occurred in 40 years, perhaps because a venue had not previously been available where both equality of power and sufficient trust existed to risk "calling a constitutional convention." The JTC was able to demonstrate that such changes to the DTA—acceptable to all sectors—are possible. For example, adjustments have recently been made to the English/communication requirement, and work is under way on the math requirements.

The role of the JTC now is to bring forward any idea, issue, or barrier that, if implemented or resolved, could further ease the transfer process for students. It was agreed that JTC members would always be "decision makers" or "policy influencers" regarding transfer issues at every institution. We have learned that when you hear a member say, "We don't do that ... ," you know that JTC membership has been assigned to someone at too low a level at that college or university. When a member says, "Hmmm, let me go back and talk with some people ... ," you know you have the right person at the table. Figure 3.1 depicts the effective process used to approve and implement change in transfer policy among Washington State's higher education sectors.

Crucial Event 6: How Can We Improve Transfer in High-Demand Majors? Heartened by the success of the AS-T degrees, in 2005 the JTC began to apply the process of developing new transfer degrees to other specific fields of study. For the first time, the overt focus of the transfer agreements became preparing students to enter and complete a chosen major, rather than simply completing general education requirements prior to transfer. Each of Washington's "major related programs" (MRPs) is based on one of the two foundational degrees (DTA or AS-T). Thus, while they prepare students for specific competitive major areas of study at the universities, they can also be utilized more generally by students whose interests change. Each MRP is selected by the JTC, and then the specific curricular requirements are negotiated by faculty members from the public and private baccalaureate institutions offering that major, along with faculty representing the community and technical colleges.

Figure 3.1. Process Used to Approve, Implement, and Monitor Transfer Policy

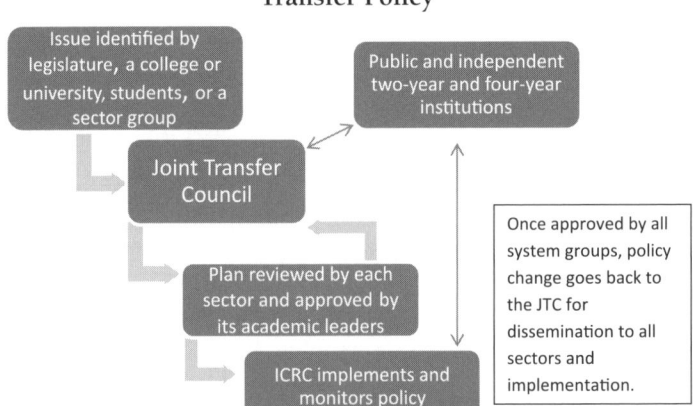

Washington State now offers 16 MRPs in areas such as nursing, engineering, business, teacher education, biology, construction management, and so forth, all created collaboratively by groups of faculty in the respective disciplines. MRPs are periodically reviewed and revised—again, by groups of faculty—in response to business and industry changes or other curriculum change associated with a program. To ensure rational development in the creation of MRPs, the JTC first determines that the major is in reasonably high demand by students; that preparation for the major in the first two years requires a substantial number of specific courses; that more than one institution awards the bachelor's degree in that field; and that the total credits earned by transfer students who graduate in the field are consistently higher than the number of credits earned by freshman-entry students in the same major.

Careful selection of disciplines based on the agreed-upon criteria is helpful. At one point, enthusiastic about this new development in transfer in Washington, the legislature mandated that additional transfer degrees should be developed each year, but experience has shown that *too many MRPs created too quickly can overwhelm community colleges, and not all of them are able to or interested in offering all of the MRPs.*

More Recent Policies to Improve Transfer in Washington

With the basic structure of transfer policy development in place, more recent refinements have come more quickly and with easier collaboration.

Technical Colleges Granted Authority to Offer Transfer Degrees (2009). Prior to 2009, graduates of technical colleges were limited to specific articulation agreements between programs at certain institutions or "upside down" degrees (degrees where discipline-specific courses are offered in freshman and sophomore years at the technical college and general education courses are offered in the junior and senior years) offered at a few public and several for-profit institutions. In 2009, technical colleges were granted authority by the legislature to offer transfer degrees—including transferable academic courses—that prepare students in professional fields such as business, health care, and engineering. The SBCTC had sought this authority for the technical colleges in the interest of students who were beginning their studies toward a technical degree, but who would benefit from the inclusion of general education and prerequisite coursework to support a later transfer. The willingness of the universities to change their policies to readily accept academic courses from the technical colleges—a significant shift for most of them—was considerably enhanced by the transfer structure in place by then, which provided positive venues for discussion based on open and positive relationships.

Student Rights and Responsibilities (2009). Although ultimately vetoed in its entirety, in 2009 the legislature had passed a bill that included a requirement for a Transfer Student Bill of Rights. In response to the veto message, as well as to fend off any further legislative action (which seemed highly likely), a work group that included all the major transfer-related groups (JTC, ICRC, SBCTC, COP, WSAC, ICW) collaborated in drafting its own Transfer Student Rights and Responsibilities and disseminating it in brochures and Web sites. Interestingly, the 1986 transfer agreement, which first enshrined the DTA in WSAC policy, included fairly similar language about student rights and responsibilities, along with a detailed student appeal process, so rights and responsibilities are not new. *If we don't pay attention to history, we are destined to repeat it!*

Associate of Science-Transfer (AS-T) Degree Guidelines (2010). When the STEM-based transfer degrees were developed, it was not entirely clear to all institutions that the degree should exempt recipients from taking all of the general education requirements at the receiving institution. This issue was elevated to JTC by the SBCTC at the request of their colleges. Thus, a 2010 agreement clarified that, while 15 quarter credits remained for completion after transfer, all the pretransfer general education courses counted toward the receiving institution's general education requirements. The clarified policy was recommended to each sector by its JTC members and, after internal vetting, endorsed as institutional policy—both individually and collectively—at the provost level by the ICAO.

Transfer Liaison (2011). A transfer liaison was established at the WSAC in 2011 at the request of the JTC, in part to be a single point of contact to resolve individual transfer students' issues and concerns, and partly in an attempt to gather better data about possible systemic issues related to transfer. Since March 2011, fourteen calls or inquiries were made to the transfer liaison—all resulted in resolution for the student. *None, to date, suggested a pattern that could be solved systemically.*

Legislation to Codify Transfer Degrees (2011). In 2011, Washington State's legislature passed a multifaceted bill intended, in part, to improve transfer education. It codified the DTA guidelines established by the ICRC 40 years ago by acknowledging in statute that a Washington community or technical college student who has earned a transferable degree is granted junior standing when admitted to a four-year institution of higher education. The transfer student is also deemed to have met (or, for AS-T graduates, nearly met) the lower-division general education requirements of the receiving institution. It required community and technical colleges and public four-year colleges and universities to publish a list of one year's worth of community and technical college courses that would transfer to all public colleges and universities *as general education requirements at the receiving institution*. While the list of courses, now titled the "Washington 45," was created and published on all relevant Web sites, the colleges did not create a formal transfer credential, as had been hoped by legislators, as it would have negatively impacted students' opportunity to continue receiving federal financial aid.

In addition, the legislation required each community and technical college to publish a list of transfer courses it offers that meet the DTA guidelines and distribution areas in order to clarify which courses will transfer most readily. And each four-year college and university now must publish a list of recommended courses for each academic major to help transfer students design their courses of study. For the most part, the 2011 legislation required more and better communication about policies and practices that were already in effect, but that were not always sufficiently apparent to the public. *Clear, consistent communication that reaches its intended audience and answers their needs for information remains a challenge everywhere.*

Secrets to Washington's Successful Transfer Model

Washington State's successful transfer structure and process is built on three—or possibly four—interdependent factors. First is an organizational **structure** that involves key decision makers representing public and independent baccalaureate institutions and community and technical colleges. The structure has been modified over time to respond to changing dynamics and needs. Second, the state has benefitted from responsible and creative **leadership** in each higher education sector committed to seeking resolution to every seemingly intractable issue that might arise; each willing to "give a little" to get more. We tend to be "nice" people up here in the Northwest!

Third, pivotal **events** that have challenged the organizational structure and the history of goodwill and tenaciousness among representatives—moments of "looking into the abyss"—have led to renewed efforts to pull back, rebuild trust, put aside institutional interests, and push forward to create new solutions and, at times, new structures.

Finally, a possible fourth factor might simply be the length of time that the original agreements have been in place—40 years—which continues to reinforce the viability and stability of collaboration and negotiation rather than either top-down mandates or go-it-alone elitism.

Future Possibilities

The JTC continues to identify issues to work on. For example, some of Washington's 16 MRPs have not yet graduated any students. This year, the JTC is investigating reasons for those MRP's nonuse and will either revise them or retire them for lack of demand. A JTC work group, composed of faculty from all three sectors, is revising the quantitative skills requirement in the DTA. Currently, the agreement requires an intermediate algebra prerequisite and five quarter credits of college-level math or other symbolic reasoning. The work group is attempting to align agreement requirements more flexibly with broad discipline pathways for business, education, and

STEM majors, majors requiring statistics (e.g., social sciences), and majors in humanities and related areas.

The JTC will also be working with system partners to review reciprocity among institutions for high school Advanced Placement and International Baccalaureate test scores and credits. And, finally, the JTC is collaborating with the WSAC on a Lumina grant that WSAC has submitted to help create a less labor-intensive and more consistent approach to retrospectively awarding transfer associate degrees.

Lessons Learned

The process of documenting the history of struggles and accomplishments in Washington's transfer education system illuminated some lessons learned:

- The characteristics and qualifications of participants in the development and implementation of transfer policy matter. The individuals who represent each sector—preferably in equal numbers—should:
  — Have the position authority to impact and influence change.
  — Be listeners who value the interests of the other constituents.
  — Be able to step out of their institutional/agency role and commit to a state policy interest for the good of the entire system.
  — Be candid and willing to lay issues out fully for discussion and resolution.
  — Always seek a solution, not a sector win.
- Transfer systems and discussions are dynamic and in continual need of improvement.
- Solutions are best when those closest to understanding the issues and barriers are involved in creating them.
- Written procedural and policy agreements among partners tend to have lasting and involved participation and oversight. Statutory and regulatory mandates tend to be checked off a list of "things to do," and tend to be less well maintained.
- Trust among participants can be rebuilt during difficult times if the foundation and history of relationships have been strong.

References

Kisker, C. B., Wagoner, R. L., and Cohen, A. M. *Implementing Statewide Transfer and Articulation Reform: An Analysis of Transfer Associate Degrees in Four States.* Los Angeles: Center for the Study of Community Colleges, 2011.

State Board for Community and Technical Colleges. *About Us.* Olympia, Wash.: Author, 2012. Retrieved August 27, 2012, from www.sbctc.ctc.edu/general/a_history.aspx.

Washington Council for High School–College Relations. *The ICRC Handbook.* Olympia, Wash.: Author, 2009. Retrieved August 27, 2012, from www.washingtoncouncil.org

/ICRC%20Documents/THE%20ICRC%20HANDBOOK%20%20updated%20August%202010.pdf.

Washington Student Achievement Council. *Transfer Task Force Transfer Agreement.* Olympia, Wash.: Author, 1994. Retrieved August 27, 2012, from www.wsac.wa.gov/sites/default/files/1994TransferAgreement-Proportionality.pdf#search ="proportionality agreement".

JANE SHERMAN *is vice provost for academic policy and evaluation at Washington State University. From its inception until this year she served as the baccalaureate-level co-chair of the Joint Transfer Council. She had earlier worked on state transfer policy as deputy director for academic affairs at the WSAC (formerly HECB).*

MICHELLE ANDREAS *is director of student services and transfer education at SBCTC. Michelle is staff to the JTC, the Instruction Commission, and a participant in the ICRC.*

4

This chapter analyzes the complex and often surprising process by which Louisiana, a small state with four higher education systems, deployed a transfer degree program in a scant two years. The author reviews the full range of challenges, from social to curricular to promotional, that were overcome and makes recommendations concerning the development of transfer degree programs under both normal and extreme or unusual circumstances.

Widening and Wandering the Short Road to Success: The Louisiana Transfer Degree Guarantee

Kevin L. Cope

Surprise is a word and concept seldom associated with higher education policy or with one of its most demanding projects, the development of a statewide articulation and transfer program. Legislators who mandate articulation enterprises and officials who care for these behemoths present themselves as thoughtful managers who cherish meticulous research and careful planning. Whether thoughtfully or not, states usually take years or even decades to develop channels through which students may efficiently flow from high school through community colleges and on to four-year universities. As enthusiasm for statewide articulation plans percolates out from large, prosperous, inventive states to smaller, lower-scoring, and less densely populated regions of the country, the pace at which transfer degree initiatives germinate, grow, bear fruit, and occasionally wilt increases. As the ferociously ontological idea that certain kinds of student fit certain kinds of schools—that some students are "state school material" while others are destined for major research institutions and still others should pass their postsecondary time in "junior colleges"—gives way to the notion that

---

Note: The author would like to express appreciation to Michael Gargano, former vice president and chief of staff of the Louisiana State University System, for help with amalgamating the chronology of and gathering other documents pertaining to the development of the Louisiana Transfer Degree Guarantee, as well as for encouraging the preparation of this essay.

students should follow any of a number of tracks through, into, out of, and possibly back into assorted campuses, the pressure to deploy articulation programs builds. As program development accelerates, the number and variety of surprises multiplies. Transfer degree programs institutionalize a commitment to acceleration by signaling that two short years is the optimal interval for determining where or whether students ought to seek four-year baccalaureate degrees. As anyone who has ever seen a wind tunnel video might suspect, each nudge, push, or shove from legislatures increases the turbulence in the transfer degree implementation processes. That is precisely the story of the surprisingly successful but ever-turbulent transfer degree program in Louisiana.

Helpful Haste and Inventive Itinerancy

A look at a sudden, minimally planned entry into the development of a transfer degree program like that which occurred in Louisiana is more than an item of intellectual interest. Small states casting about for quick fixes want to solve old problems quickly. Development of articulation programs may occur only a short time prior to their mandated implementation, allowing no time for a trial period. Influential legislators or statewide regulatory entities may call for such programs at any time, whether or not local tradition or previous groundwork warrants them. To put it paradoxically, intelligent haste, the opposite of the usual academic deliberation, is required, whether in assembling the array of committees needed to do the job with a semblance of academic credibility or in recruiting the small cadre of somewhat more expert persons who can complete the project on time.

The first surprise in the articulation development process is that which comes to those who will create the transfer degree program. These colleagues may be known for their public-spiritedness or for their interest in curriculum but may never have heard of articulation. Startled by being selected, they may experience uncertainty with respect to expectations and may doubt the wisdom of the undertaking. The number of qualified professionals who both command respect among academic colleagues and who also understand articulation will also be small, with disorientation and a sense of inadequacy among participants being the result. Smaller still is the cadre of academicians who are not members of schools of education— whose status as experts within disciplines is required to lend credibility to the program.

In the spring of 2009, the Louisiana legislature passed its Act 356 (http://legis.state.la.us/billdata/streamdocument.asp?did=449955), which mandated the establishment of a 60-hour portable degree by which students at any state higher education institution who complete the stipulated hours, who meet general education requirements, and who follow designated curricula may automatically earn admission to any four-year state university in

Louisiana at the junior (third-year) level. Sponsored by a well-meaning, avuncular legislator who had completed a two-year technical college curriculum but who had little direct experience of four-year institutions, Act 356 abounded in exhortative optimism but stipulated a short schedule while delivering few specifics and minimal guidance.

I quickly found myself among the surprised upon discovery that I had been appointed to chair the key General Education subcommittee of the new Statewide Articulation and Transfer Council. That sudden promotion may not be as unusual as it may seem. Having served for several years and during a time of intense economic crisis as faculty senate president at the state flagship research campus and also as chair of the system-wide council of faculty advisors, I had had the opportunity to work with the nomenklatura of higher education management and to sojourn with state officials while also continuing to resemble a faculty member from a liberal arts discipline. Being enough of an insider to be "known" but having links to the legitimizing academic world made for a good match with an initiative that would have to take a top-down, high-speed approach to dealing with widely dispersed institutions and interest groups. It might be said that the available role made the would-be expert rather than the expert making the role. My colleagues on the Council and among its many working groups also perceived themselves as having fallen into their roles.

The first lesson for those developing transfer and articulation programs is, then, the urgency of quickly maximizing peripheral talent: talent that seems to fit enough of the bill to do the work but talent that might come from elsewhere in the labyrinth of higher education than traditional management. After all, articulation and transfer programs are largely concerned with *general* education and with *varied* institutions. Some of this talent will be outright scruffy and unaccustomed to the slick style of consultants and other capitol crawlers. A related lesson might be that haste and surprise allow policy-focused system chancellors or presidents to foster leaders whose aptitudes correspond to the generality of public education—who can connect the highly pragmatic attempt to generate more associate degrees with the traditional goals of university education and who can therefore help to communicate the good news concerning higher education and upward social and cultural mobility to uninitiated audiences.

Step one in the development of a transfer degree program is thus the acceptance of an inevitability: that the personnel who will create the program very likely have slid into rather than studied for their roles. A follow-on step is quietly but honestly recognizing who will be the players in the articulation game, a recognition that requires acknowledging that few of those largely political influences that will enter the process will conform to the customs or expectations of educators. With so much variety as well as suspicion at play, literally—physically—getting out of the office box and moving off administrative turf will help to set the program in motion. In a state such as Louisiana, where the population is thin, the campuses dispersed, and the four management systems endowed with multifarious institutions fulfilling assorted, often overlapping role-scope-mission statements, direct, face-to-face discussion on neutral ground helped to jump-start the process and to overcome fear and territorialism. Given that General Education accounts, in Louisiana, for 39 of the 60 hours that comprise the transfer degree, summoning as many General Education experts as were willing to travel from all of those campuses that offer undergraduate instruction seemed a good opening strategy. Contrary to widespread belief among alienated faculty members, those working in the abstracted world of system offices are usually eager to win faculty consent to their initiatives from campuses hither and yon and to ensure that those initiatives meet accreditation requirements for faculty input. With the blessing of the Louisiana State University (LSU) System, I called a meeting in remote and rural Eunice, Louisiana, at an LSU System campus that also happens to be a highly productive two-year institution. Holding the opening meeting of General Education experts in a context that would likely produce a large number of the two-year transfer students had a galvanizing effect, giving meeting participants a sense of and appreciation for their project while reminding campus representatives that the major stakeholders already had a high level of agreement with regard to the proper content of those 39 General Education hours.

The Prestige Paradox: Envious Institutions Moving Students Up the Quality Ladder

Higher education systems are not created equal. Transfer and articulation generally occur across system lines and in an upward direction on the ladder of prestige. Students proceed from community colleges to regional universities or from regional campuses to research institutions or occasionally from state into private colleges. Differences in prestige, rank, and suitability for career preparation tend to make one system in a multisystem state the most frequent target for transfer degree earners. The transfer process is also asymmetrical across time. Very few holders of associate degrees later transfer back from four-year institutions to pursue additional two-year credentials. In practice, that one system that takes an initial leadership role or that arranges consultations such as the aforementioned Eunice conclave quickly gains the advantage in managing discussions and creating the framework for the transfer program. This advantage is largely a matter of institutional culture and has little to do with the suitability of any set of institutions for receiving transfer students. In Louisiana, for example, the University of Louisiana System includes more four-year campuses than does the LSU System, yet the LSU System led the discussion and provided the framework for the emerging program, in large measure owing to its research emphasis and habit of innovation. The Southern University and University of Louisiana Systems, with their tradition of teaching and service, tended to collect data and to take a reactive approach to suggestions from the LSU System—an approach that served political purposes but that seldom affected the proposed programs.

A lesson to be learned from this experience is that the representatives of a "receiving" system that students regard as a highly desirable destination need to balance leadership in the transfer program development process against the protection of self-esteem among representatives of less prestigious campuses and systems. A recurring theme in the Louisiana discussions was respect for and recognition of the value of community college courses. Low wages and poor working conditions along with a shortage of faculty holding doctoral degrees in Louisiana community colleges increased sensitivity among council members to the point that robust, honest evaluation of community college offerings became all but taboo. Negotiating long-standing antagonisms, rivalries, and occasionally jealousies involved repeatedly affirming that community college instruction carried a definite and measurable value, while also assuring stakeholders in four-year universities that transfer and admission standards would not decline. Representatives of systems in the middle tiers—one, a historically black colleges and universities (HBCU) system; and one, a system of regional and small research institutions—tended to disappear from a largely emotional dialogue between the ambitious and the service institutions. They sympathized with the difficulties of colleagues in two-year institutions but also sought to preserve standards that they regarded as essential to their traditions. This sense of being slighted or otherwise overrun by powerful institutions plays no small part in the way that transfer degree programs evolve.

Negotiating a transfer degree program in a multisystem state is thus a complex social process. Success at the task requires attention to the business and administrative traditions of systems that often have very different styles, a task made all the more difficult by the unfamiliarity of faculty experts with the habits of top-level university managers. In Louisiana, the LSU System tended to work through short summit conferences in neutral venues that looked at the fundamentals of transfer programs while the University of Louisiana System created an elaborate network of data-compiling committees that took a rather more empirical and distributed approach to decision-making. The community college system, by contrast, fielded a cadre of administrative experts to argue for its positions but seemed never to consult faculty members. The Southern University System sought out faculty opinion but often had trouble finding participants. The frequent meetings of the Statewide Articulation and Transfer Council thus looked populous and followed defined agendas, yet conflicting administrative, ideological, and occasionally educational currents were always circulating (or colliding) beneath the visible surface. Progress depended on an unstated collective resolve to wade through those currents, indeed to pretend that they did not exist.

Omission of data sometimes proved more important than information gathering. The gathering of information requisite to the development of a transfer degree program makes for an interesting study of the interaction between the apparently information-saturated environment in which professional educators work and the social and organizational constraints under which state agencies labor. Until recently, the Louisiana Board of Regents, which maintains the Transfer Degree Guarantee program, did not manage to post any information relating to this initiative online, although the information is now available (www.latransferdegree.org/index.html). In addition, although members of the Statewide Articulation and Transfer Council received e-mail minutes of Council meetings, a search for the myriad documents used in or generated during the development of the program is fruitless. Under Louisiana law, all documents pertaining to the program are matters of public record, but researchers must make a request for them—a classic "Catch 22" situation in which one must know the information before seeking the information. It is unlikely that the online information desert pertaining to the Transfer Degree Guarantee developed from ill will. More likely is that such a program, by crossing department and agency boundaries and by decreasing the overall regulatory burden, lacks an archival home in an agency with sharply drawn command lines and tight administrative structure.

Whatever the deficiencies of Louisiana's information-distribution system, too careful a consideration of institutional and system-level differences could poison the atmosphere. Many, if not most, states evidence some sort of geographical and cultural divide, for example, that between northern and southern California or that between Manhattan and upstate New York. In Louisiana, the physical distance between northern and southern population centers (and university towns) as well as an assortment of long-standing cultural divides (e.g., between the southern, Catholic-influenced and northern, Protestant-dominated regions or between "Cajun" western Louisiana and metropolitan cultures of Baton Rouge, New Orleans, and Shreveport) amplified the potential for distrust. As the development process continued, it again became clear that a discussion on neutral ground with representatives from all systems and many campuses might break deadlocks. The solution was a consultation in yet another, even more obscure and ecumenical facility: a learning outreach center housing satellite programs for several universities that is located in the center of the state, in Alexandria, in a converted building on a former military base. The discovery that an array of otherwise competing university systems maintains the equivalent of a "safe house" in a remote region is certainly one of the most peculiar outcomes of a transfer degree development exercise. Traveling to neutral ground in a central location not only showed goodwill but also built community spirit, with the adventure of voyaging to a largely unknown place functioning as a team-building exercise. Owing to the thrift and efficiency that characterizes academic culture, the value of such team-building exploits in advancing a project is easily underestimated, especially in our era of compressed video and e-mail communication. The few occasions on which video conferencing was attempted showed the contrary result, increasing alienation and confusion and demonstrating that off-site, in-person discussions increase efficiency and deliver good value for money.

Other methods for reducing tension and increasing productivity may be more subtle and may involve the unconventional use of faculty resources to accomplish policy goals. In an effort to reduce the tensions along the most problematic and polar opposition, that between the LSU System, with its research-oriented campuses, and the Louisiana Community and Technical College System (LCTCS), where production of student credit hours and attainment of credibility top the list of goals, I invited the LCTCS vice president to address the LSU Faculty Senate and to explain the role and also market niche of Louisiana's two-year schools, a gesture that pleased the faculty at the major research university while producing a significant change for the better in interactions on the Statewide Articulation and Transfer Council. Surprise, in this case an unprecedented invitation, lubricated a process that was always on the brink of breakdown owing to the stiffness in administrative machinery.

General Education: A Common Transfer Currency of Unmeasured Value

When the Statewide Articulation and Transfer Council began its deliberations, the Louisiana Board of Regents mandated 39 hours of General Education (GE) coursework distributed over six disciplines. Arithmetically, the GE component would thus account for the majority of the credit in a 60-hour transfer degree. So large a GE requirement can be a blessing as well as an encumbrance insofar as it limits options. Devoting two thirds of the required coursework to GE decreases both the choices available to and the confusion among students. It constrains the range of possible dissent, thereby frustrating inventive colleagues but also reducing contention. Two consequences arose from the large allocation to GE. First, the principal Transfer Council members, the four vice presidents of the four university systems, recognized that the GE subcommittee, composed exclusively of faculty members with assorted areas of disciplinary expertise, would emerge as the starters within the transfer team. General education would be the core of the transfer degree enterprise. Second, the remaining 21 hours, divided between "common course prerequisites" that were explicitly prohibited from functioning as gateways to specific concentrations and colleges, and elective "subject areas courses" became difficult to define, being neither general (per "general" education) nor specific (per the prohibition against specific prerequisites). Curiously, the statewide GE requirements do not appear on the Louisiana Board of Regents' Web site, but they are identical with those in force at LSU (www.cae.lsu.edu/genedhome/).

Academicians may be notorious for promoting their own disciplines without concern for the general curriculum, yet determining the content of the GE portion of the Louisiana transfer degree proved far less challenging than the procedural, political, or structural arrangements for this offering. For one, the statewide regulatory body, the Board of Regents, had already partitioned knowledge into disciplinary areas (such as humanities, fine arts, and sciences). The strict—some might say old-fashioned—inventory of disciplines minimized controversy. Even those who wondered whether, say, "composition" ought to count as an independent "area" could not dispute the notion that mandated composition classes should produce writers capable of penning grammatical sentences. Even those with esoteric ideas could not deny that, once the idea of a "finite mathematics" has been admitted, college students taking such a course should master the rudiments of algebraic operations. Instead, quarrels erupted over whether the GE component of the transfer degree should prepare students for what cynics might call "general admission" into a university—admission into very broad areas such as the humanities or the sciences without guaranteed access to particular senior colleges—or whether the transfer degree curriculum should lay out tracks leading into specific concentrations.

The stakes in this debate were twofold: emotional and jurisdictional. On the emotional side, a track system appealed to the representatives for community and regional institutions in that tracks suggested the credibility of their coursework. Guaranteed admission into senior colleges or selective disciplines would signal that students had received adequate, respectable instruction. Automatic admission into a selective college within a four-year university affirmed that junior colleges had come of age. The research campuses, however, looked on the development of "tracks" and the associated automatic admission into particular programs as attempts to bypass entrance examinations and thereby to evade measurement of the quality of community college instruction. At stake, too, was possible usurpation of faculty control over admissions standards and curricula.

On the policy or jurisdictional side, the enabling legislation, Act 356, guaranteed no more than admission into a four-year university, saying nothing about entering selective colleges or programs. The uncertainty about what the Transfer Degree Guarantee actually guaranteed threatened to weaken its market appeal. In the end, the cleanness and simplicity of the broader, less specific area approach prevailed. The prospect of developing dozens of tracks for dozens of disciplines proved daunting. Anecdotal evidence suggested that naive students, many of them first-time college-goers from rural parishes, were not prepared, at the age of 17, to commit to an overly deterministic track. Eventually, and largely as a political concession, tracks for popular disciplines such as criminal justice or nursing were later deployed. The political and therefore harmless character of such concessions is indicated by the lack of evidence that any students are following those tracks.

En route to the consolidation of transfer degree options into a few procedures for broad areas, a number of ugly scenes arose, in part owing to the reluctance of some two-year colleges to disclose sample syllabi, some of which turned out to be less than one-half page long. A lesson to be learned from this phase of the transfer degree story is that inadequate acquaintance with institutional mission, clientele, and context begets paranoia. The reason that community college syllabi are short is that the sometimes desperate conditions under which community college instructors in poor states work and the low level of college readiness among students together make flexibility necessary and rigor difficult. A 10-page syllabus touching on every cultural figure from Martin Luther to Jackson Pollock is probably too stiff for the pertinent student clientele. Refusal to admit to or to explain the dilemma of motivated but obstructed community college teachers increased suspicion more than it built respect.

A similar mix of emotional investment and policy preoccupation swirled around the government agency charged with managing the transfer degree, the Louisiana Board of Regents. In Louisiana, the Regents' responsibility is legally limited to planning, provision of standards (such as admissions minima), data collection, budgeting, and research. De facto, however, the Regents supervise a large but diffuse range of initiatives that would find neither encouragement nor administrative domicile elsewhere—including initiatives such as the Louisiana Transfer Degree Guarantee. The trouble that arose, however, is that, as a regulatory agency, the Regents had earned a reputation for reluctance with regard to innovation and for an excess of bureaucratic procedures. Midlevel officials in the Regents office had long maintained a complicated articulation matrix that included not only a bewildering number of spreadsheet cells but that also featured no less than 38 footnotes that, in turn, abounded with exceptions and qualifications to the supposed rules. "The matrix," as its acolytes reverently called it, resisted interpretation by all but seasoned educators. It routinely staggered first-time college-goers in Louisiana's rural parishes. Upon my appointment as chair of the GE subcommittee of the Transfer Council, I selected as my first mission the dismantling of the matrix and its replacement with a far simpler descriptive list of both eligible and exemplary courses. The matrix provided no guidance for future course development; a more fluid list would provide a qualitative indication of the kinds of courses that might qualify for GE transfer credit. Flexibility would be key for a program that aimed specifically at the production of baccalaureate degrees without respect to field of study and that would need to account for new courses, especially in the scientific or technical areas. Months of debate ensued, but, in the end, the "list" approach carried the day.

The lesson here is threefold. First, professorial colleagues seldom anticipate what might be called "bureaucratic superstitions" such as the cult of the matrix that thrived in the statewide education authority. Second, success in creating a program that stipulates flexibility requires flexible media, such as lists, rather than hard and minimally adaptable instrumentation such as an intricate articulation matrix. A third lesson is—again—that venues really do count. Those negotiating programs must consider the environment in which discussions proceed. Where one does the work can be as important as what one does. Louisiana educators would have spent far less time debating the merit of an obviously unusable matrix if the meetings had not been held in the Regents' office and in the presence of Regents' staff but had instead rotated around sundry campuses.

Outcome of the Debates: The Transfer Guarantee

Before looking at the audience reception of the Louisiana transfer degree, it may be useful to summarize what emerged from the development process. From the months of debate came a kind of genial imprecision regulated by quantitative componentry. As previously explained, the transfer degree adheres to Louisiana Board of Regents regulation by mandating 39 hours of general education and by stipulating that those hours will be distributed according to an unambiguous formula: 6 hours of English composition; 6 hours of mathematics or analytical reasoning; 9 hours in the sciences, including a 6-hour sequence in either the biological or the physical sciences; 9 hours in the humanities, including 3 hours in the study of literature; 6 hours in the social and behavioral sciences; and 3 hours in the fine arts. Although this arrangement recalls a traditional "distribution requirement" that lacks a focus and may be little more than a loose basket for gathering student credit hours, the program enforces a degree of coherence by mandating a sequence of two courses in the physical sciences and by placing literature, perceived by Louisiana's students as one of the more difficult humanities offerings, at the center of the liberal arts requirements. Additionally, students must consult with an advisor and choose a "track" that will lead to another 21 hours of study that, although not strictly allocated to disciplinary prerequisites, nevertheless orients students toward further study in one of the large areas of knowledge, whether the sciences or the humanities or the arts (or several others). The program also varies from the traditional "distribution" model by not mandating any set of specifically identified courses but, rather, declaring criteria by which counselors may determine whether a course qualifies for inclusion in the transfer degree curriculum. The resulting blend of generality and specificity provides the flexibility needed for the very wide range of students entering the Louisiana system while it helps a minimally prepared student population adapt to the traditionally partitioned landscape of knowledge that it will encounter upon arrival at four-year institutions. A guide for advisors replete with program details is available online (www.latransferdegree.org/TDGAdvisorsGuide2010.pdf).

The Audience for Articulation

The question of venue is also the question of audience. Newcomers to the development of large-scale, intersystem, multicampus, statewide transfer programs focus more on the content of curricula than on the presentation of those programs to the vast audience composed of the public. The enabling legislation for the Louisiana transfer degree expressed large ambitions along with an admixture of impatience but offered little guidance with regard to implementation, funding, or promotion. The result: in-house conversations yielding a call for proposals from public relations firms, a call coupled with high expectations but low support. The obscurity of state bidding procedures and the introversion of state agencies made it difficult for faculty associated with the Louisiana transfer degree campaign to explain to professional extroverts such as advertising account executives what in the world the desired promotional materials should express. Predictably, the selected public relations firm, an in-state company, made a series of false starts. That firm, for example, tended to thematize, both graphically and with regard to content, peripheral and para-academic ideas. Although it did not appear in the colors of any state school, green was selected as the dominant hue for the Web site and for printed materials owing to the alleged trendiness of "green" ecological concepts among young people, a claim for which no evidence appeared. Extremely conservative designs festooned the first portfolios, as if the consultants sought to fend off criticism; in one layout, members of the advertising firm appeared as supernumeraries in the imagery, disguised as (somewhat senior) students. Relying solely on the power of media, the consultants advanced no plans to contact high school counselors or to meet with community groups in the field. Television spots had to be revised owing to a biracial approach—one advertisement was directed to white students and another version of that same advertisement was directed to black students—that several council members considered retrograde. Small quantities of printed materials were produced, but tracking their distribution has proved puzzling. A statewide traveling show that would bring news of the program to selected campuses commenced but gradually diminished without the reporting of results and without completion of the itinerary. It is all too easy to criticize a public relations firm with no experience in large-scale higher education initiatives that is trying to deal with inconsistent input from state officials. What is presently most needed to advance the transfer degree program is an intense, comparatively low-tech, grassroots program that would involve visits with high school and preparatory school counselors, mobile vans parked at shopping centers and other public venues, and widely distributed printed matter such as brochures and flyers. Higher-end electronic media such as Web sites and occasional television spots will have trouble overcoming the unfamiliarity, in Louisiana, of both the transfer degree program and higher education generally. Sadly, funding for such face-to-face efforts is in short supply.

Also underestimated was the territorial behavior of officials at individual campuses. More than a few campus chancellors and presidents reacted to the emergence of the Louisiana transfer degree by negotiating their own, sometimes impromptu "2 + 2" plans with nearby community colleges. Those community colleges, seeing a promotional opportunity, embraced this somewhat subversive option. Faculty also tend to fear reductions in the supply of students and so seldom speak out against local administrations in favor of the statewide approach. Faculty require more education about the value of statewide student streams in maintaining enrollment in disciplines in which step-by-step progress is required such as the science, technology, engineering, and math (STEM) fields or the foreign languages.

The intersection of transfer degree programs with public constituencies brings with it—to invoke again the keyword for this essay—surprises. One surprise is that interest groups both inside and outside the educational community resist the generality of the GE component of a transfer degree even when that broader educational experience promises to raise the prestige of a program by transforming it from a vocational to a collegiate offering. Despite the prohibition against consuming the 60 hours of transfer credit with prerequisites for specific concentrations, many, if not most, transfer students are seeking entry into "accredited" fields such as nursing or engineering in which the choice among courses may be so constrained even in the early years of an education as to make compliance with the transfer degree curriculum impossible. During the development of the Louisiana transfer degree, several councils were called—of nursing school deans, of engineering deans, of business deans—to cut through this Gordian knot. My own position as someone without a formal administrative position allowed for the congregating of such synods; there being no precedent of an interloper arranging such discussions, few ready-made objections were at hand. Again, sheer unexpectedness served a worthy purpose. Groups of discipline- but not institution-affiliated deans who were accustomed to dealing in-house with discipline-specific accrediting associations were more than a little surprised to find themselves working through the elementary arithmetic of 60-hour programs even while wondering how they got to the meeting in the first place. The sense of wonder increased morale and thereby rendered these discussions far more productive than might be expected. These and many other ad hoc consultations quickly produced tracks that could fit within a program dominated by general education.

Less successful but also less awkward was the outreach to private colleges and universities, which, in Louisiana, have banded together in their own organizations: the Louisiana Association of Independent Colleges and Universities (LAICU). The extreme variety of LAICU, which includes HBCUs, an allied health college, wealthy private institutions, and even a religious seminary, rendered its integration into a streamlined program all but impossible. Underestimated as well was that very small segment of the academic public that sits on courses-and-curriculum committees and that often resents outside regulation or implementation of programs. And with good reason, for accrediting agencies mandate that faculty control curricula, an expectation that a statewide transfer program could easily violate. Those refractory faculty members often forget that student credit hours generated by articulation-ready courses can greatly benefit colleges.

Anyone embarking on service to a transfer degree development committee should prepare for a variety of spinoff tasks that occur in the public eye. Testifying to legislative committees becomes almost a routine matter. The skills required when addressing the diverse body of legislators that one encounters in a small state do not come naturally to academic professions. In Louisiana, only a subset of state legislators have completed college. One Louisiana legislator, for example, farms alligators; another sells reclining chairs. Elementary distinctions, like that between GE and ordinary courses, must be explained simply and speedily but without patronizing overtones. At the opposite end of the audience spectrum are state-appointed commissions addressing vast projects such as the restructuring of higher education, commissions composed of experts and data enthusiasts who quickly weary of the kind of broad responses suitable for legislators. Faculty members who testify before state officials generally do so through or at the behest of an intermediary or superior; hence the cultivation of good relations with higher education commissioners or state secretaries of education or similar leaders can make a significant difference in the initial reception of testimony. Prior introduction by a ranking state official makes the difference between being taken seriously and being dismissed as yet another egghead activist. Many high-ranking officials emerge from cultures very different from that of academe. Faculty shepherding statewide programs must adapt to a pace, style, and variability that differs from the deliberative pace of scholastic exchanges.

Coda: Dangerous Success Is Nevertheless Success

Once a transfer degree program that is rich in GE opportunities is established, the challenges become all the greater as legislators or management board officials discover other, not always altruistic opportunities. In Louisiana, both legislators and Board of Regents officials are now aspiring to move from transfer degree programs to common course numbering initiatives that veer far from the General Education heritage of statewide articulation and that bode fair to produce the kind of cumbersome regulation and large bureaucracies that transfer degree programs curtail. Statewide articulation of any kind threatens the identity of institutions. Students transferring from school to school may not develop the same sense of loyalty or the same habits of alumni giving as those who commit to a four-year education in one venue. Transfer degree programs have a natural appeal to nontraditional students and can be of use to emerging urban universities such as Portland State and the University of Wisconsin at Milwaukee, yet both Louisiana's advertising campaigns and the pathways that program participants are actually following suggest that the adult cadre is being overlooked. Perhaps sadly, most transfer students continue to come from the usual pool of 18-to-24-year-old near-traditional students.

The fact that state-level decision makers enjoy meddling with transfer degree programs demonstrates *a fortiori* that transfer degree programs are successful. When lawmakers experience temptation, there must be tasty bait. Admittedly, the start-up period in Louisiana has been slow. To date, roughly three transfer degree students have graduated from a four-year institution. In the pipeline, however, are nearly 700 students who are nearing the baccalaureate degree and who have reasonable prospects of graduating on schedule. That Louisiana should accomplish this in but three years, amidst a major economic downturn and flight of talent out of state, may well count as miraculous.

KEVIN L. COPE is president of the faculty senate at Louisiana State University and is chair of the LSU System Council of Faculty Advisors. Since early 2009, he has been chair of the General Education Subcommittee of the Louisiana Statewide Articulation and Transfer Council. He is also a member of the "SATC" Subcommittee on Common Course Numbering.

This chapter outlines how Ohio developed a comprehensive, guaranteed transfer system that connects colleges and universities, high schools, adult career centers, and the workplace. Ohio's story confirms the importance of clearly defined pathways, faculty-determined course equivalency, cutting-edge technology, and effective, determined leadership.

Faculty-Determined Course Equivalency: The Key to Ohio's Transfer Mobility System

Paula K. Compton, Jonathan Tafel, Joe Law, Robert Gustafson

For more than two decades, the vision of a statewide system of student mobility has driven Ohio's articulation and transfer initiatives, which guarantee that specific courses will be applied to degrees and certificates at public two- and four-year postsecondary institutions. Since 1991, Ohio students have been guaranteed transfer credit for the Ohio Transfer Module (OTM), a subset or a complete set of each public college or university's general education requirement. Initially, students who completed the entire OTM at one institution received credit for the OTM at the institution to which they transferred, thereby completing most, if not all, general education requirements. Since 2002–2003, each individual course in the sending school's OTM has been applied in the corresponding area of the receiving school's OTM without requiring that students complete the full OTM.

In fall 2005, Ohio increased students' opportunities for guaranteed credit transfer by implementing Transfer Assurance Guides (TAGs). TAGs go beyond the OTM, focusing on requirements in a given major, including prerequisite and introductory courses. Unlike OTM courses, which guarantee application simply to an area of general education, TAG courses are guaranteed to apply to specific course requirements within a degree program. For example, in the Communication TAG, a course identified as *Small Group Communication* at one institution will transfer as *Small Group Communication* at any Ohio public school offering the communication major—no matter what the course title or number at either school. As of early 2012, there were 42 TAGs in 8 discipline areas, comprising more than 3,500 approved course matches across the state.

Ohio's transfer guarantees extend beyond the courses taken at two- and four-year postsecondary schools. Since 2009, any Ohio student attending an Ohio public institution of higher education who scores a 3 or higher on any of the Advanced Placement tests available from the College Board will be awarded college credit in accordance with statewide guidelines, often credit for OTM or TAG courses. The most recent initiative, Career-Technical Credit Transfer (CTAGs), is a collaborative effort involving the Ohio Board of Regents (OBR), the Ohio Department of Education, public adult and secondary career technical education, and state-supported institutions of higher education to give college credit for agreed-upon technical programs/courses based on industry standards and in many cases passage of a third-party credential. More information about these transfer initiatives, including links to all approved course matches, is available on the Credit Transfer page of the University System of Ohio (USO; USO Board of Regents, 2012).

These statewide initiatives have had a clear impact on Ohio's students. In 2010–2011, 42,998 undergraduates transferred within the USO, an increase of 43.4 percent since 2002. These numbers are especially impressive because Ohio's colleges and universities are not part of a fully integrated higher education system like those found in New York, Wisconsin, North Carolina, and other states. Even after a governor's executive order established the USO in 2007, Ohio's colleges and universities continued to have substantial autonomy and independent boards of trustees that are responsible for institutional policies and operations. Remarkably, the statewide transfer initiatives have preserved institutional autonomy while guaranteeing the application of transfer credit at any state institution. This transfer system is the product of collaboration across the state, involving legislators, the OBR, and administrators and faculty from Ohio's 14 universities, 24 regional campuses, and 23 community colleges. This chapter surveys the evolution of this system, focusing on the concepts of equivalency and campus ownership, and concluding with a discussion of the hallmarks of Ohio's transfer system.

Evolution of the Ohio Transfer System

Ohio's articulation and transfer reforms date from 1988, when the Ohio General Assembly directed the OBR to develop a statewide mechanism to allow students to transfer credits when they moved from the state's technical and community colleges to its universities. The study commission formed in response to this mandate resulted in the creation of the Ohio Articulation and Transfer Policy, which was grounded on three principles:

1. Transfer and native students should be assured equitable consideration and treatment.

2. Students who began their collegiate studies at a community college or university regional campus should be encouraged to complete an associate of arts or science degree before transferring to a baccalaureate institution.
3. Institutional autonomy and integrity for the general education program at each college and university should be assured.

In the long run, this third principle has proved to be critical. Until the USO was established in 2007, the OBR was a coordinating board with limited authority, not a governing board, and operated through collaboration and consensus building. This mode of policymaking paved the way for today's statewide guarantees that permit seamless transfer while preserving institutional autonomy. In the process, the educational culture about credit transfer that historically was institutionally focused, rather than student centered, has changed radically.

The Ohio Articulation and Transfer Policy that was created in 1989–1990 focused on general education. Even though general education is central to the curriculum and students take a majority of these courses in the first two years of college, courses associated with general education often are problematic in the credit transfer process. Working together with the Articulation and Transfer Advisory Council, which was established in conjunction with the 1988 policy, the Regents developed parameters for including courses within the OTM and a system by which representative faculty would review and approve general education courses for the OTM.

The creation of the Advisory Council was a crucial step in developing Ohio's credit transfer agenda, and it has continued to provide both leadership and oversight in the ongoing evolution of the system. As early as 2000, the Regents and Council had begun developing guidelines for transfer of credits beyond the core general education curriculum. Thus, in 2003, when Ohio's legislators initially sought to address continuing barriers to effective transfer by mandating that *all* coursework transfer and apply regardless of discipline, level, and institution, the Regents' staff already had guidelines in place and worked together with legislators to forge legislation that created a *universal course equivalency classification system* for credit transfer in Ohio. The result was the development of TAGs, which provide students with a pathway into the major. A more detailed account of the development of these initiatives can be found in *Bringing Down the Silos* (Tafel, 2010).

As the responsibilities of the Regents and the Advisory Council have evolved over the years, the membership of the Council has grown to include representatives from all of the state's public colleges and universities, the state association of independent colleges and universities, K–12 school districts, the Ohio Department of Education, and adult career programs. It is co-chaired by the presidents of a public university and a community college, and an oversight board functions as an executive committee. At the same time, transfer initiatives involving the Advisory Council and the Regents have expanded beyond the OTM and TAGs to include overseeing the transfer of credits from other types of institutions (such as adult and secondary career-technical centers), awarding of college credit for military training and experience, developing statewide standards for awarding national credit-by-exam programs, and creating electronic tools to expedite the review of course equivalencies, facilitate transcript exchange, and automate credit transfer.

To ensure the institutionalization and continued support of this work, in December 2010 the chancellor of the OBR issued a directive that created the Ohio Articulation and Transfer Network (OATN), a consortium of Ohio's public institutions of higher education. In this directive, the OATN was charged to "effectuate the transfer of students within the University System of Ohio, maintain quality assurance of courses, continue to expand the number of courses guaranteed to transfer, continue to develop transfer electronic tools, and continue to expand the transfer initiatives" (University System of Ohio, Board of Regents, 2010, p. 2). The structure and responsibilities of the OATN are shown in Figure 5.1.

Establishing Course Equivalency

Ohio's transfer guarantees are made possible through the concept of *equivalency*—establishing and matching agreed-upon learning outcomes for each course or learning experience. It is imperative that equivalency be established by faculty, who are the stewards of their discipline's curriculum. Thus, campus faculty "own" the system by which equivalency is established. Indeed, faculty-vetted equivalency is the central building block in Ohio's student mobility.

The process begins with the development of an entire transfer pathway. As TAGs were being created in 2003–2004, the Regents initially identified commonly offered disciplines for the project. They then gathered faculty from each discipline from across the state to determine the common premajor and beginning major courses for each discipline, to ascertain the potential courses that would carry the statewide transfer guarantee, and to establish the learning outcomes of those courses. For professional programs with outside accreditation, consensus was accelerated by recent moves to outcomes-based assessment that is a critical part of accreditation renewal. Additionally, basing a course equivalency system on consensus-developed learning outcomes has led to clarification across areas where needed, such as differentiating between engineering and engineering technology programs.

More recently, the process has been streamlined. Now, when a new TAG or CTAG is being considered, the Regents consult with a curriculum area expert from one of the USO institutions, who conducts preliminary

Figure 5.1. Ohio Articulation and Transfer Network

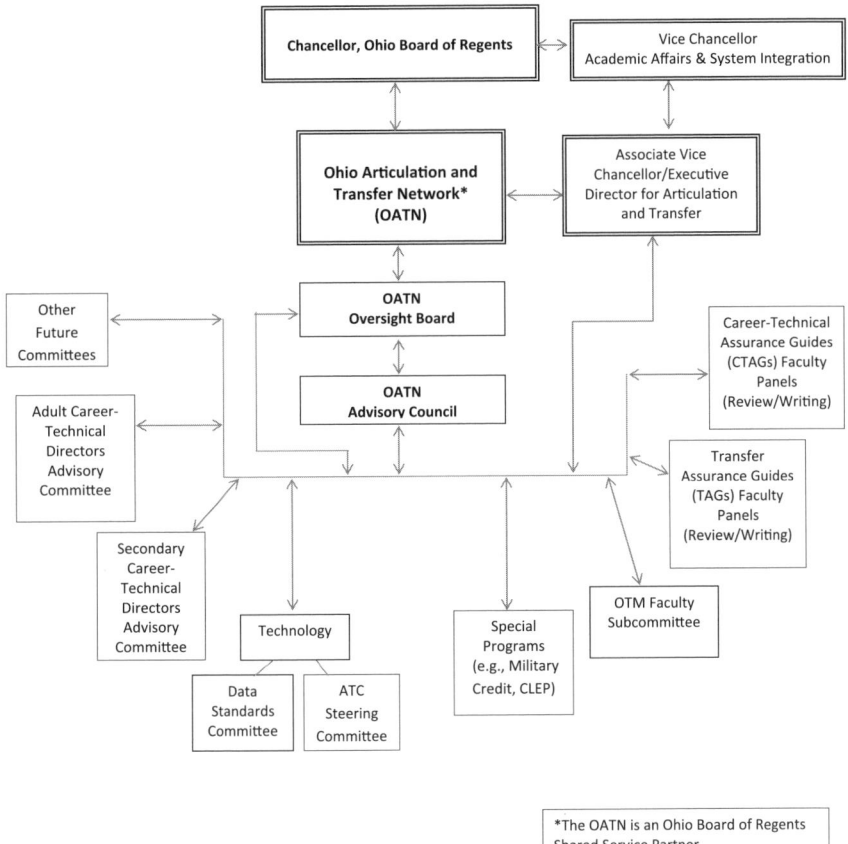

research. After identifying the commonly offered premajor and beginning courses in the discipline/career pathway in question, the curriculum expert consults with USO institutions while drafting learning outcomes and credit hours for these courses. If analysis continues to support the new TAG or CTAG, then each course within the TAG/CTAG will be developed using the following process.

Defining. A faculty content expert, often the one who carried out the preliminary research for the new TAG or CTAG, will be identified as the leader of a faculty panel that will be created for that transfer pathway. He or she will present the learning outcomes drafted during the initial inquiry to the faculty panel as a starting point for their further work. The panel will reach consensus on the draft of learning outcomes for each course in the transfer pathway and determine which are essential for a course to be considered equivalent. The panel will also decide whether all learning outcomes must be met for equivalency or whether a minimum of 70 percent will be sufficient (including all learning outcomes identified as essential). For example, within the Education TAG, the course called *Introductory Child Development* is identified as a three-hour course with seven learning outcomes, all considered essential. The Business TAG includes a course called *Business Communications*, a three-hour course with nine learning outcomes, five of which are designated as essential. In this instance, a course that addresses these five essential learning outcomes and at least two of the other four could be considered an equivalent course. In this initial step, the faculty panel also considers the credit hours for the given course and any credentials associated with mastery of the learning outcomes. Much of this information will have been gathered while the TAG/CTAG was being drafted, expediting the process. The learning outcomes that have been drafted (including recommended credit hours and credentials) during this stage will then be sent to USO institutions for endorsement.

Agreeing. Once the faculty panel has developed learning outcomes for the agreed-upon courses in a transfer pathway, an electronic survey containing those outcomes is sent to each USO institution, and a faculty member from that discipline responds to the survey questions. The survey provides an opportunity for additional faculty to give valuable feedback and to take ownership of the process. Institutional faculty may, for example, suggest clarification of the wording of a learning outcome or challenge the OBR faculty panel's designation of an outcome as essential. After results are analyzed by the OBR staff and the faculty panels, learning outcomes are adjusted, and the process is repeated until consensus around the learning outcomes is attained.

Matching. Once learning outcomes for each course in a transfer pathway are finalized, institutions identify their own courses addressing those learning outcomes and with the appropriate credit hours and degree of rigor. If an institution does not have a suitable course, they may modify an existing course or, in some cases, develop a new one. The legislation that resulted in the creation of TAGs specifies that OBR policies must "require state institutions of higher education to make changes or modifications, as needed, to strengthen course content so as to ensure equivalency for that course at any state institution of higher education" (Ohio Revised Code, 2003). Once the course has been identified, institutions submit course materials (e.g., a syllabus, textbooks used, assessment procedures, lab requirements) to the appropriate OBR faculty panel to review the match.

Reviewing. Standing panels of discipline-based faculty experts drawn from Ohio's two- and four-year campuses evaluate course materials to ensure that they meet the specified learning outcomes with the appropriate degree of rigor. If the faculty panel approves the course as equivalent, the course is then listed in the statewide course equivalency system and has a statewide transfer guarantee. If a submission is not approved, the course is sent back to the institution with suggestions for revision, and it will be resubmitted for a subsequent review cycle. For instance, a course submitted as a match for *Introductory Child Development* would have to be a three-hour course, and the materials submitted must demonstrate that students are asked to achieve the seven designated essential learning outcomes, indicate that an appropriate amount of time is devoted to each outcome, and show how student learning is assessed. A submission that did not clearly demonstrate that a course is equivalent would be returned to the institution, with a request for additional information or that it be revised in order to attain course equivalency.

A Statewide Structure of Collaboration

As this brief account indicates, the process of determining course equivalency for TAGs and CTAGs requires the support of all USO institutions. Because college and university presidents and provosts/chief academic officers back Ohio's transfer policy, they devote resources to make these initiatives a reality. Many institutions make articulation and transfer the responsibility of a high-level administrator, who serves as a liaison between the Regents and the institution and also coordinates efforts on campus. These administrators may be responsible for introducing the statewide transfer initiative(s) to faculty in a way that will gain their confidence and support. They may work with unit heads to identify faculty to participate at one or more stages of the development of a transfer pathway. These faculty will then respond to preliminary surveys concerning possible new pathways, work with other faculty across the state to develop course descriptions, and/or serve on statewide faculty review panels. When a pathway has been developed, the administrator will work with local faculty to submit the appropriate courses for review. If courses are not approved as submitted, the administrator will likely facilitate faculty revision and resubmission of the courses.

In addition to working with faculty on academic issues, the administrator will work with offices on campus to ensure that approved courses from other institutions are transferred and applied appropriately. The administrator may, for example, work with admissions offices and registrars to ensure that each approved TAG course for every other USO school is equated with that school's approved TAG course; likewise, any OTM course without an exact local equivalent must be applied appropriately to the requirements of the general education program. To do so requires monitoring Regents' reports for each review period and ensuring that all newly approved courses are properly encoded in the degree audit system. Finally, the administrator will occasionally need to work with the Regents and other institutions to resolve questions about the application of transfer credit, whether as a receiving or sending institution.

Undoubtedly, the most important form of institutional support comes from the dedicated faculty who are the backbone of Ohio's transfer system. Institutions invite their most respected faculty members to provide state-level leadership both to develop transfer pathways and course learning outcomes and to review courses against those outcomes. Over the past seven years, more than 800 faculty members have been involved in all aspects of these transfer initiatives.

When faculty are needed, academic officers are asked to nominate faculty to meet a specific request. For each curriculum domain, faculty from the broadest array of institutions across the state are selected on the basis of their knowledge of curriculum and willingness to collaborate to develop and refine each framework. Although this initially required a large number of facilitated face-to-face sessions for each subject area, this painstaking procedure respected the faculty's role as keepers of the curriculum and established the academic credibility of the initiatives. These meetings have the secondary benefit of developing rapport among faculty from the various institutions who might otherwise have no forum for discourse on curriculum in their respective areas.

Hallmarks of Ohio's Articulation and Transfer System

Ohio's Articulation and Transfer System is a complex system with many dynamic segments. A number of key factors have contributed to the successes achieved in the state.

Ohio Benefits from Strong Legislative Support. The leadership and support of the General Assembly were critical factors in accomplishing a *guaranteed* articulation and transfer system for the state. The OBR was instrumental in developing and fostering this relationship, which is reflected in legislative recognition of the faculty's role in creating and maintaining transfer initiatives. As the statewide work of articulation and transfer advanced to meet legislative directives, what had begun as a contentious relationship developed into broad-based support in the form of legislation, continued funding, and directives that provided clout to achieve the state's goal of a universal course equivalency classification system.

Ohio's Transfer Initiatives Are Student Centered and Faculty Driven. If there is a lesson in Ohio's experience that is transferrable to other states and situations, it is the necessity of direct and continuous involvement of campuses and faculty in the design and implementation of credit transfer policy. Without this involvement, progress cannot be sustained. Faculty maintain the integrity of the transfer process by giving endless hours of their expertise to sustain an ever-expanding comprehensive statewide course equivalency system to help students reach their highest level of academic attainment.

It Is All About Relationships Built on Trust. Ohio's comprehensive statewide articulation and transfer system rests upon a solid foundation of trust. It has taken time for various cultures in community colleges, universities, adult career-technical institutions, and secondary institutions to come together and develop trusting relationships and partnerships. The development of this trust has been gradual, originating in the collaboration among the Regents and representatives of all the state's public institutions in the creation of the OTM. The same respect for faculty authority that established the academic credibility of the OTM was further expanded during the creation of TAGs and CTAGs. Additionally, the Regents have begun follow-up studies concerning the academic preparation of students who have taken advantage of these transfer guarantees, and early findings demonstrating these students' success will enhance faculty confidence in these initiatives.

Technology Plays a Key Role. In the early development of transfer initiatives, work was done entirely with hard copies of syllabi and in-person meetings. Now with the help of the Course Equivalency Management System (CEMS), work is done electronically. Faculty from around the state submit course matches online, and members of faculty panels review those submissions and report back in the same way. Faculty still meet in person when they wish and have conference calls, but the bulk of their work is done using CEMS. Regents staff have developed in-person and virtual training programs for each of the state's key transfer initiatives for both faculty and administrative staff. For the public, interactive reporting systems have also been created to provide information about the statewide transfer guarantees for OTM, TAG, CTAG courses, and Advanced Placement scores. Users can view equivalent courses in any category for each USO institution. One additional information system should be noted. Early in the development of the state's credit transfer initiatives, the Regents and the Advisory Council worked with Miami University (in collaboration with Arizona's Board of Regents) to create and implement a Web-based advising tool that encompasses not only courses with statewide transfer guarantees but bilateral transfer equivalencies between individual institutions. Originally known as the Course Applicability System (CAS) and now known as u.select, it provides an online mechanism for transfer advising and credit transfer equivalencies. The Ohio Revised Code requires that all state institutions fully implement a course applicability system.

Ohio's System Is Flexible and Adaptable. The articulation and transfer system continues to evolve, as indicated in the earlier description of changes to the organizational structure, processes, procedures, and policies. As trends in employment, education, and student demographics continue to change, the OATN is responding by developing new statewide guarantee initiatives. The number of TAGs and CTAGs continues to grow, and the OTM transfer guarantee has been strengthened by the development of OTM courses with specific learning outcomes. Transfer pathways and individual course learning outcomes will be reviewed periodically to stay current with curriculum developments and accreditation standards and to ensure that the appropriate degree of academic rigor is maintained. The Regents have also launched research projects to track the academic success of students who participate in these initiatives, and the results of that research and of the periodic review of existing initiatives will allow all parties to enhance and strengthen TAG and CTAG design.

Ohio's mobility system works because it puts students at the center of a faculty-driven process and gives them tools to navigate the postsecondary system to achieve their highest educational aspiration.

References

Ohio Revised Code. *Universal Course Equivalency Classification System for State Institutions of Higher Education*, 2003. Retrieved Sept. 17, 2012, from http://codes.ohio.gov/orc/3333.16.

Tafel, J. *Bringing Down the Silos: A Primer on Credit Transfer and Student Mobility.* Columbus: Ohio Board of Regents, 2010. Retrieved Sept. 17, 2012, from http://regents.ohio.gov/transfer/documents/bringing-down-the-silos.pdf.

University System of Ohio, Board of Regents. *Credit Transfer.* Columbus: Ohio Board of Regents, 2012. Retrieved Sept. 17, 2012, from www.ohiohighered.org/transfer.

University System of Ohio, Board of Regents. *Re: Establishment of the Ohio Articulation and Transfer Network* (Directive 2010-045). Columbus: Ohio Board of Regents, 2010. Retrieved Sept. 17, 2012, from http://regents.ohio.gov/actions/documents/2010/dir2010-045.pdf.

PAULA K. COMPTON *is associate vice chancellor, articulation and transfer, Ohio Board of Regents, and executive director, Ohio Articulation and Transfer Network.*

JONATHAN TAFEL *is emeritus vice chancellor for academic affairs, Ohio Board of Regents, and president, Sycamore Street Consulting.*

JOE LAW *is assistant vice president for articulation and transfer and professor of English at Wright State University.*

ROBERT GUSTAFSON *is director, Engineering Education Innovation Center, and Honda Professor of Engineering Education at The Ohio State University.*

6

This chapter describes how California Community College and California State University faculty developed a system for implementing associate degrees for transfer that has the potential to simplify transfer and decrease unit accumulation. This intersegmental, faculty-led system provides a mechanism for maintaining local control of curriculum, while identifying curricular commonalities that can ultimately facilitate student movement within and between higher education segments in California.

Faculty Reflections on Implementing Associate Degrees for Transfer in California

Jane Patton, Michelle Pilati

In 2010, California's then-governor Schwarzenegger signed Senate Bill 1440, called the "Student Transfer Achievement Reform Act" (Padilla, 2010), into law. This bill mandated that the state's 112 community colleges (CCCs) develop a new type of associate degree, an "associate degree for transfer," that specifically prepares a student for admission to the California State University (CSU) with certain guarantees after transfer. The legislation did not specify how the degrees should be developed, making it possible for faculty to take responsibility and propose a concerted, coordinated approach to implementation that would ensure that the college and university faculty remained in charge of the curriculum and yield additional benefits for students not envisioned by the legislation. This chapter will summarize the system that has been created for developing these new associate degrees, discuss the circumstances that facilitated the development of a systematic response, and reflect upon the lessons that can be drawn from the first two years of implementation in a state with 135 community colleges and state university campuses.

The Call for Associate Degrees for Transfer in California

Nationally, colleges and universities have been soundly criticized for the low numbers of degrees attained by students both at the community college and university levels. Along with the rest of the country, California has felt pressure from the legislature and from internal educational leadership to promote a completion agenda. A task force on transfer in California (Transfer Task Force, 2009) concluded that the state needed transfer associate degrees, and a report from the Center for the Study of Community Colleges summarized salient viewpoints of task force members and highlighted the circumstances that would be needed in order for statewide associate degrees to be realized (Kisker, Cohen, & Wagoner, 2010). Many of those recommendations informed legislation that was subsequently drafted. In 2010, the chancellors of the CCC and the CSU joined forces and identified the improvement of transfer and degree attainment as one of their highest priorities, and they began working with the legislature to effect Senate Bill 1440, which in essence mandated the creation of transfer associate degrees in California.

In considering the impact of any statewide initiative in California, one must recognize the state's complexity and the unique challenges and opportunities that complexity creates. California's system of public higher education consists of three independent segments with specified missions and target populations. The University of California (UC), with its 10 campuses, enjoys complete autonomy from the legislature. The CSU has 23 campuses, and the CCC system consists of 112 colleges in 72 autonomous college districts governed by local boards. The CSU and CCC systems are independent from each other, and both are subject to regulation by the state legislature. The legislature has repeatedly tried to regulate coordination between the CCCs and the CSU in an effort to streamline transfer with limited success.

While various factors can make transfer challenging, when SB 1440 became law, California already had in place two important features to ease movement between systems of higher education. First, the state had two well-established general education patterns for transfer: the CSU General Education-Breadth Requirements and the Intersegmental General Education Transfer Curriculum (IGETC), a transfer pattern that is accepted by both CSU and UC. At the lower division, CSU GE-Breadth consists of a 39-semester unit pattern. Transfer students must take approved courses in these areas: English Language Communication and Critical Thinking, Scientific Inquiry and Quantitative Reasoning, Arts and Humanities, Social Sciences, and Lifelong Learning and Self-Development. The requirements for IGETC are similar, requiring student completion of courses approved in prescribed areas and a minimum of 37 units. Completion of either transfer general education pattern is "certified" at the community college prior to transfer.

In addition to its two general education (GE) patterns, California also had a statewide articulation resource called ASSIST (Articulation System Stimulating Intersegmental Transfer) in place prior to the passage of SB 1440. ASSIST is "an online student-transfer information system that shows how course credits earned at one public California college or university can be applied when transferred to another" (www.assist.org/web-assist

/welcome.html). ASSIST makes existing articulation agreements readily available not only to higher educational professionals, but also to students, parents, and the general public. While ASSIST provides a resource to determine what coursework a student needs to complete at a given CCC for transfer to a specified major at a specified UC or CSU, it also perpetuates a system that requires students to prepare differently for transfer to different institutions, even within a given major. In other words, the student who wishes to prepare for the sociology major at three different CSU campuses may need to satisfy three different sets of requirements.

Put simply, while students wishing to transfer from a California community college to a university have long had a clear pathway with respect to completing the general education component of their transfer preparation, they have always faced a challenge when it comes to completing major preparation courses due to many differences in requirements at the various CSU and UC campuses. In addition to the different requirements of the various transfer destinations, the curriculum of every community college is unique. Furthermore, the range and content of associate degrees offered varies widely. While some community colleges have a wide array of degrees designed to facilitate transfer, others offer degrees in transfer majors that are not aligned with transfer requirements, and still others offer very broad degrees that rely on appropriate student course selection to prepare the student for transfer. The lack of alignment between local associate degree and transfer requirements provided no incentive for degree completion before transfer and potentially led to the accumulation of many more units than necessary in order to both complete a degree and transfer. Concerns about the complexity of transfer, student unit accumulation, and the lack of associate degree completion were all factors that prompted a broad array of constituent groups to support and advocate for Senate Bill 1440.

Senate Bill 1440 required each community college to begin to offer new associate degrees for transfer to the CSU system beginning in the fall 2011 term. As the legislation did not specify how many degrees must be offered, but effectively mandated more than one (the plural "degrees"), the CCC Chancellor's Office determined that at least two degrees at each college were required in order to be compliant with the law as of the fall 2011 deadline, with the expectation that colleges would develop more degrees later. In addition to specifying benefits for students upon transfer, the law stipulated certain requirements for the associate degree for transfer: degrees must require no more than 60 semester units or 90 quarter units (for simplicity we will refer only to semester units as this system applies to all but three community colleges in California); degrees must include the completion of a transfer general education pattern and a minimum of 18 semester units in a major or "area of emphasis" (an "area" is like a major, but broader); degrees shall not include any additional local graduation requirements such as ethnic studies or physical education.

The legislative restrictions placed on the CSU—and resulting guarantees for students—included the following:

- Students applying to the CSU with the associate degree for transfer must be accepted somewhere in the 23-campus system into programs that are deemed to be similar.
- Students must be able to complete a baccalaureate program in 60 units beyond the associate degree.
- Students shall not be required to repeat courses that are similar to those already taken.

While the UC system was not included in SB 1440 and is not subject to regulation by the Legislature, it is common practice to *encourage* its participation where appropriate, and another bill was passed in September 2010 (AB 2302; Fong, 2010) requesting the UC to consider developing transfer pathways with the community colleges.

Setting the Stage for Success

In their analysis of the implementation of associate degrees for transfer in four states, Kisker, Wagoner, and Cohen (2011) identified seven elements of effective transfer degree programs; a number of these were directly addressed in SB 1440: credit applicability, junior status upon transfer, guaranteed university admission, and associate and bachelor degree credit limits. While their report was published in April 2011, after California had passed SB 1440 and had designed its system for associate degrees, it is remarkable how much the state's implementation reflects the conclusions in the report. Senate Bill 1440 did not contain *all* of the report's recommendations, however. In particular, the bill did not provide for a clear organizational structure. Further, it did not mandate the development of a coordinated system nor direct the two systems of higher education to work together. Thus, what *could have* happened in response to SB 1440 and what ultimately *did* happen are two quite different things.

What Could Have Happened in Response to SB 1440 (and What Did)

Because SB 1440 did not mandate a coordinated solution, California's 112 community colleges could have developed 112 different degrees in each transfer major, and then each college would have needed to seek acceptance of these degrees from each of the 23 CSU campuses. This approach would have fulfilled the letter of the law, but would not have simplified the transfer process and would have created a new bureaucracy with no benefits to any constituency. Luckily, California's faculty are represented locally and at the state level by elected academic senates. The existence of these state-level faculty bodies permitted system-level conversations about SB 1440 prior to its passage by the legislature. As its passage appeared imminent, the faculty worked to influence the final language of the bill and began discussions of how it should be implemented long before it went into effect on January 1, 2011.

Early conversations among representatives from the two academic senates led to a clear consensus that the best way to implement SB 1440 would be through a well-coordinated, faculty-driven, statewide approach. Previous statewide efforts and legislation aimed at strengthening the transfer process had failed partly because the implementation processes were not developed intersegmentally. Although SB 1440 put the authority for the development of associate degrees for transfer explicitly in the hands of the community college faculty, the two academic senates recognized that it was in the best interest of students and both systems if intersegmental discipline faculty groups established a consensus-based model that delineated the major preparation needed for transfer.

Thus, in April 2010—five months before SB 1440 was signed into law—discussions began regarding the development of a statewide response to SB 1440. The two academic senates organized an ad hoc group of college and university faculty from transfer disciplines along with college faculty in articulation and counseling. In addition, representatives from both Chancellors' Offices were invited. In these early ad hoc meetings in the spring and summer of 2010, the idea for developing a statewide, faculty-developed system for the implementation of SB 1440—as opposed to individual transfer degrees for each of the 112 community colleges—was conceived.

After SB 1440 became law, the CSU and CCC chancellors formed an SB 1440 Implementation Oversight Committee, which included appointees from their offices, the academic senates, campus administrators, and students. The oversight committee meets regularly to discuss issues and concerns regarding the implementation of the degrees. However, early on it was agreed that this committee would not address the academic and curricular matters, leaving those instead to the two academic senates. Consequently, the faculty-led ad hoc group evolved into the Intersegmental Curriculum Workgroup, and was formally charged with implementing and overseeing the curricular elements of the legislation.

One of the first priorities for the CCC faculty was to determine what the new degrees would be called in order to distinguish them from existing associate degrees, many of which had been designed for transfer but were not consistent with SB 1440 requirements and, therefore, were not subject to the restrictions and benefits conferred by SB 1440. Thus, the label "associate degrees for transfer" was added to the lexicon of the CCCs. Majors in the STEM disciplines, as well as the Career Technical Education fields, would be called AS-T (associate in science for transfer) degrees, while all other majors would be AA-T (associate in arts for transfer) degrees.

Associate Degrees for Transfer and California's Course Identification Numbering (C-ID) System

Over the past few decades, assorted laws and regulations had aimed at improving intersegmental transfer in California, with various levels of success. Several laws required the segments to adopt "common course numbering," and after the previous California Articulation Numbering System was discontinued, the Academic Senate for the California Community Colleges began developing a new system to address this mandate. When SB 1440 became law, the structure in that system became the backbone of a concerted approach to developing the new associate degrees for transfer. Using a statewide system for degree development meant that it was necessary to have a means of identifying comparable courses within these degrees. Fortunately, the numbering system introduced in 2006, the Course Identification Numbering System (C-ID), was intended to address the call for common course numbering and would also provide a means of identifying comparable courses. When SB 1440 was passed, C-ID was an existing system in the initial stages of full implementation that could be used to describe the courses that would be included in associate degrees for transfer.

C-ID is based on a system of robust course descriptors that can serve as both the basis for articulation and as a standard that courses to be granted a C-ID designation must meet. Receiving institutions indicate their willingness to accept courses that match a given C-ID descriptor in lieu of a course requirement at their campus. In doing so, all courses that receive that C-ID designation are granted the descriptor-based articulation. In short, C-ID offers a mechanism for "one-to-many" articulation; institutions interested in articulating with all of the state's community colleges can choose to articulate with the C-ID descriptor, effectively then granting articulation to all courses that match that descriptor.

Central to the work of C-ID is the convening of a small group of college and university discipline faculty, appointed by their statewide academic senates, to develop detailed course descriptors for the common transfer courses in their discipline. These descriptors include course content, objectives, assignments, and textbooks and provide assurances to receiving institutions about the skills and knowledge students will gain. Draft course descriptors are vetted for statewide input via an online system (www.c-id.net). Finalized descriptors are distributed to the universities where the faculty determine whether they will accept courses that match the descriptors in lieu of their local courses. Community colleges then submit their official course outlines of record to a committee of intersegmental faculty who determine whether their courses sufficiently match the descriptors, and when they do, the course is granted a C-ID designation. When a community college submits a course for a C-ID designation, it is also agreeing to accept courses with that designation, effectively establishing intrasegmental articulation.

Thus, when SB 1440 was signed into law and the community colleges were tasked with developing new associate degrees for transfer, the infrastructure for implementing a statewide response was already in place through C-ID. The C-ID system of intersegmental faculty collaboration could be used to draft statewide model curricula for the transfer degrees, and drafts could be vetted online, allowing for statewide input and buy-in from all constituencies. The C-ID structure ensures that California's associate degrees for transfer are developed through faculty-driven processes.

Transfer Model Curricula—The Key to Coordinated Implementation of SB 1440

As the previous paragraphs illustrate, when SB 1440 was passed in 2010, many of the elements necessary to develop a statewide system for associate degrees for transfer were in place, including transfer general education patterns (IGETC and CSU GE-Breadth), ASSIST, and most importantly, a process for identifying comparable courses and intersegmental collaboration (C-ID). Building on these foundations, the CCC and CSU academic senates set out to create what they called a Transfer Model Curriculum (TMC) for each of the most popular transfer majors. These TMCs would include the courses that intersegmental faculty deem most appropriate for both transfer preparation and an associate degree in a specific major or area of emphasis. Each TMC would be created using the intersegmental, faculty-driven C-ID processes and would be vetted by faculty throughout the state. Furthermore, the perspectives of transfer and articulation personnel would be taken into account, and each community college would be able to develop an AA-T or an AS-T that aligned with the TMC for that discipline. The TMC process thus simplifies local degree development by providing a framework for associate degrees for transfer. TMCs also ensure expedited approval by the CCC Chancellor's Office, as the main components of each TMC-aligned degree have been, to some extent, predetermined.

In October 2010, less than a month after SB 1440 was signed into law, the C-ID system hosted faculty discipline group meetings in the northern and southern regions of California and invited faculty from more than ten disciplines to begin to draft TMCs and their associated C-ID course descriptors. In the subsequent three months, faculty in three disciplines were able to vet and finalize TMCs, and in January 2011, the first three TMCs were completed in communication studies, psychology, and sociology. The TMC development process is detailed below.

The TMC and Degree Development and Approval Process

California's process for developing and aligning courses with TMC consists of the following steps.

Discipline Faculty Develop a TMC. The process of developing a TMC begins with both academic senates appointing discipline faculty to be members of a Faculty Discipline Review Group (FDRG). Each group is charged with two primary tasks: to identify the courses that could and should be in a TMC and to draft and vet course descriptors for those courses using the C-ID processes. In order to encourage widespread perspectives and input on the model curricula, a number of larger "come one, come all" discipline group meetings were held during 2010–2011 and 2011–2012 for faculty to brainstorm preliminary TMCs and course descriptors.

TMCs Are Vetted. Once a draft TMC and its associated course descriptors are developed, they are vetted. Discipline faculty and transfer personnel from both segments are encouraged to go online (www.c-id.net) and provide constructive criticism of the model curricula. This process provides information as to the relative availability of courses at the CCCs and the significance of certain courses at the CSU.

During the initial phase of TMC development, dramatic changes in TMCs after online vetting were relatively rare. This was likely due to the broad array of input provided and the disciplines that were selected. More often than not, concerns were raised during the vetting that the FDRG had already considered. For example, a research methods course is required in the Psychology TMC. Because slightly less than half the CCCs offer such a course, many respondents during the vetting objected to the inclusion of this course as a required component of the TMC. However, more than half of the CSUs with the major require it, and many CCC faculty similarly believe it would not be appropriate to offer a degree in psychology without such a foundational course included. It was important to explain this rationale once the vetting concluded and the TMC was finalized.

Following the vetting period, the FDRG reviews the vetting input and makes revisions to the drafts as needed. If the drafts have significant modifications, subsequent vetting is conducted. Once the FDRG is satisfied that the TMC represents a consensus of the discipline, it is subject to a review by the Intersegmental Curriculum Workgroup to ensure that established guidelines were followed. The process for developing corresponding C-ID descriptors is simpler: once the FDRG is satisfied with vetted course descriptors, they are officially approved and are posted on the C-ID Web site.

TMCs: Finalized for Use. Finalized TMCs are posted on the C-ID Web site and are sent to the CCC and CSU Chancellor's Offices. The CCC Chancellor's Office then develops the necessary forms for colleges to complete (a "TMC Template") when seeking state approval for their TMC-aligned degrees. The creation and use of the template simplifies the degree submission and approval process. When the CSU Chancellor's Office receives a finalized TMC from the C-ID office, a staff member sends it to each CSU campus where the departments are asked to determine whether a student who has earned an AA-T or AS-T that is aligned with the TMC could complete his or her baccalaureate program in 60 units (per SB 1440).

As the legislation required CSUs to accept students somewhere in the system into "similar" programs, the word *similar* was operationally defined as baccalaureate degree completion being possible within 60 semester units. In some cases, the CSU departments immediately determined their degrees were similar; in other cases the faculty concluded that the TMC-aligned degrees did not sufficiently prepare students such that a student could complete the BA or BS in 60 units. When that occurs, the CSU Chancellor's Office asks the departments to reconsider their determination, and reportedly, some CSU's are modifying their curriculum in order to be able to accept a given TMC. The determinations of "similar" status are regularly reported on the sb1440.org Web site.

Status of TMC and Degree Development. During the first year of SB 1440 implementation (2010–2011), the focus was on developing the infrastructure for a statewide system and ensuring that all 112 community colleges had at least two SB 1440–compliant degrees in place for fall 2011. The Academic Senate for California Community Colleges worked with the CCC Chancellor's Office to provide webinars, workshops, and informational materials to college faculty and staff to assist them in developing and seeking approval of TMC-aligned associate degrees for transfer. By the end of the 2010–2011 academic year, most colleges were on their way to offering one or more of the new degrees. At the same time, more Faculty Discipline Review Groups had been formed and were developing TMCs and the corresponding C-ID course descriptors.

During academic year 2011–2012, more discipline groups were formed, and by December 2011 the state had 16 TMCs. In addition, C-ID descriptors were in place for most of the required courses in the finalized TMCs. By June 2012, there were 20 TMCs in place (with four more anticipated in the near future), and 420 AA-T and AS-T degrees had been approved by the CCC Chancellor's Office.

The focus for academic year 2012–2013 is on increasing the number of TMC-aligned degrees offered, finishing the C-ID descriptors for at least 25 majors, and considering a mechanism for TMC-development for disciplines not selected for TMC development on the basis of their popularity as a transfer major. It has been estimated that when the top 25 majors have TMCs, close to 80 percent of transfer students will be able to pursue their chosen transfer major by completing an AA-T or AS-T degree. In addition, several Career Technical Education disciplines, even though they may not be among the "high transfer" disciplines, have expressed interest in participating in the TMC development process.

In the first year of transfer degree implementation, the C-ID infrastructure supported and facilitated the work of the faculty meetings, but it was increasingly evident that additional funding would be needed. Fortunately the CCC and CSU Chancellor's Offices had submitted a grant proposal to Complete College America, a nonprofit organization focused on increasing the numbers of college certificates and degrees in the country. When the grant was awarded to California in autumn 2011, it supported the completion of TMCs for the top 25 transfer majors and the necessary rapid expansion of C-ID to develop course descriptors for all of the courses in the TMCs. The grant also supported the development of strategies for marketing the new degrees to prospective students. This timely infusion of funds from Complete College America was vital to the full implementation of SB 1440.

Overcoming (Most) Challenges in Implementing Associate Degrees for Transfer

Not surprisingly, a number of challenges regarding the development of associate degrees for transfer have surfaced, but many have been resolved. One early challenge was differing perspectives on what a degree should consist of; there were some people who believed a degree should be designed to be as easy to achieve as possible, while others held that it must represent an academic achievement based on a common minimum academic standard. Because these were degrees in specified academic disciplines, the Academic Senate for California Community Colleges asserted the right of the discipline faculty to establish minimum standards for their discipline. Creating degrees that were comprehensive enough to constitute an associate degree in a given discipline and were consistent with the requirements for transfer required a balance between sometimes competing interests between faculty in the discipline and faculty in student services. The differences were overcome largely because of the structure being used: intersegmental discipline faculty ultimately determined the content of degrees.

Developing a TMC-aligned degree sometimes required the development of new curricula at the CCCs. At a time of unprecedented fiscal crisis, when course offerings were being dramatically reduced, many colleges were understandably reluctant or unable to develop new courses. In the psychology example cited earlier, efforts to develop a research methods course that could be used by a variety of disciplines (and therefore be a course the college would be more likely to have the capacity to support) were not successful. This course remains an issue for the psychology discipline, and a few similar challenges may exist in other areas. While this dilemma is not yet fully resolved, one possible mechanism for addressing the issue may be through ensuring universal availability of such courses through distance education.

The public higher education system in California lacks an oversight body to serve as the ultimate arbitrator of disputes and decisions. As implementation progresses, this situation may become even more of an issue. While the Implementation Oversight Committee meets regularly, it is not a regulatory body and generally provides a forum to share progress and discuss issues that have arisen. Furthermore, the independence and autonomy of the CSU campuses and the CCCs create an opportunity for policies that vary at the local level. The leaderships of both systems have very limited authority over local institutions that choose to operate in a manner inconsistent with the legislation and the statewide implementation. Nonetheless, the Implementation Oversight Committee has established goals to be met by both systems, and the leadership of both have worked toward the achievement of these goals. The established processes for transfer degrees are working well in some areas of the state and are less effective elsewhere; some CCCs have only developed the two degrees required for initial compliance with SB 1440, and the CSUs that have always opted to be more selective are hesitant to make the compromises required by this effort.

As with most initiatives, sustainability is a concern. While the CCCs were, essentially, pressured to declare that SB 1440 would not be an unfunded mandate, implementation does have costs at both the local and state levels. An ongoing financial commitment is required to sustain what has been created. In a state with rapid legislative turnover, it will become increasingly important to educate the legislature about the efforts in place and the cost savings they promise.

Transfer reforms do not happen overnight. A report from the independent Legislative Analyst's Office (2012) was generally supportive of the implementation system, yet cautioned about the limited extent to which the degrees are in place. *Reforming the State's Transfer Process: A Progress Report on Senate Bill 1440* concluded that (1) the TMC system was an effective solution and should be expanded, (2) more colleges needed to develop more AA-T and AS-T degrees, and (3) more CSU programs should accept TMC-aligned degrees. At this time, whether these recommendations will be realized absent additional legislation is unclear.

The creation of the TMC system has brought discipline faculty to the table, and that has raised some universal academic questions, such as who owns the lower division, which courses really belong in the lower division, and whether the units of some courses have been expanded over the years in ways that prevent containment of the number of units students accrue. SB 1440 clearly aimed at reducing the time to degree and the number of units required in degrees, yet in some disciplines, courses that used to be three semester units are now four or five units. These questions have been asked but not yet answered.

Lessons Learned

As we reflect on the implementation of SB 1440 and California's associate degrees for transfer to date, we have learned several things.

Ensure a Faculty-Driven Approach and Utilize Existing Transfer Infrastructure. The faculties of California's autonomous segments of higher education are sometimes maligned as an obstacle to effecting change in a state with the two largest systems of higher education of their kind in the world. In truth, however, the nature of higher education in California has actually fostered the development of structures, relationships, and policies that facilitated the statewide response to SB 1440. The existence of strong and effective statewide academic senates allowed the faculty of the two segments to lead a coordinated approach and garner widespread support from colleagues. The academic senates of all three segments of public higher education meet regularly as the Intersegmental Committee of the Academic Senates (ICAS). ICAS provides a forum for the CCC and the CSU to share their progress and has prompted UC to consider how they, too, could participate. UC has recently announced that the associate degree for transfer is one of their eligibility pathways, and the UC will guarantee a comprehensive review of the applications of students holding the AA-T and AS-T degrees, making the degrees advantageous to students seeking to transfer to UC (California Community Colleges Chancellor's Office, 2012). UC's willingness to participate would have been unlikely had their faculty leadership not only been aware of the publicity surrounding this initiative but also privy to the ongoing issues and progress.

Another factor that has contributed to the climate for success is the fact that the CCC and CSU faculty had already been actively collaborating on C-ID (while efforts have been made to include UC in the work of C-ID, UC's participation has been minimal to date), providing the foundation for the statewide approach to the development of associate degrees for transfer and the infrastructure for statewide collaboration. Finally, the approach that the faculty took to this new initiative was to learn from past successes and failures, and the structure that was developed overcame various errors from previous efforts. Curriculum is within the faculty purview, and therefore this component of the initiative had to be divorced from the administrative components. Because California's higher education system is not "top-down" and both the CCC and CSU academic senates enjoy relatively effective relationships with their respective Chancellor's Offices, the faculty asserted this operating principle early on and it was not questioned. In order for this effort to succeed, faculty had to take the lead.

Establish Universal Buy-In as a Goal. We found that universal buy-in must be recognized as a goal, not as a foundational assumption. Every effort must be made to address as many criticisms as possible but to not expect that every aspect of the system will automatically appeal to all parties or be universally accepted. Some constituencies will not recognize the benefits of the system until they have been proven over a long period of time. The concerns of all groups must be taken into consideration and addressed to the greatest extent possible but should not be permitted to act as an impediment to progress.

Ensure Clear Communication. Communication is critical both within each segment and intersegmentally. Any breakdown in communication can result in a loss of confidence. Within the CCC system, we found that explaining the structure of a given TMC and why certain choices were made within it went a long way toward addressing concerns about the TMC and assisting the field in understanding how the TMC should be used when constructing a degree. It was critical that decision-making processes were explicitly shared and that responses to concerns expressed in the vetting were considered.

Even more important is effective communication between the segments. An example of a communication misstep was CSU's announcement early in 2012 that it would only accept transfer students who had completed one of the transfer degrees (AA-Ts and AS-Ts) for a particular term, creating concern among disciplines without such degrees and concerns that transfer degrees would soon be the only transfer pathways. The CCC had no forewarning about this announcement, so it resulted in system-wide alarm. Had the CSU informed the CCC of the reasoning behind the edict that was delivered, the CCCs could have forestalled some of the panic. Unfortunately, the announcement was received as an indication of what is to come in the future—that the *only* transfer students to be accepted must hold these degrees—when in reality it was a reasoned response to the state's current fiscal crisis. Campus funding had been reduced and programs curtailed, but the CSU is obligated by SB 1440 to admit students with the associate degrees for transfer. The legislation mandates that these students are *guaranteed* a place in the CSU system; if registration is open for a given term, students who have an associate degree for transfer must be accommodated.

Create and Document Processes for Developing the Degrees. All processes that are put into place regarding the development of transfer degrees should be documented to the greatest extent possible. The system must also be open to changes as needed, but all changes should be justified based on clear principles. While early efforts may require action absent a defined progress, clear documentation is needed not only to communicate to others, but also to ensure all necessary safeguards are in place. Guiding documents facilitate the effective communication that is so critical to success.

Conclusion

California's Student Transfer Achievement Reform Act (SB 1440) did not mandate the development of a coordinated system, and it did not direct the faculty of two systems of higher education to work together. However, the system that was implemented is highly coordinated both within and between the segments. Ultimately, the approach taken not only serves to fulfill the mandates of SB 1440, but furthers prior legislated efforts related to common course numbering and common major preparation, yielding a system with more benefits for students and the state than initially envisioned.

The system that was eventually put into place not only met the letter of the law, but it also created a coordinated system to identify appropriate lower division preparation for common transfer majors. It forced faculty to the table to determine appropriate curricular pathways, it has increased the number and variety of degrees being offered at the CCCs, and the expectation is that it will increase the number of associate and baccalaureate degrees earned. However, to be sustainable, the system will require maintenance. California must assume responsibility for providing the ongoing resources and funding necessary to sustain the collaborative system if the transfer degree initiative created by SB 1440 will be able to achieve its full potential.

References

California Community Colleges Chancellor's Office. *What Counselors Need to Know about AA-T, AS-T Degrees.* Sacramento, Calif.: Author, 2011. Retrieved Sept. 17, 2012, from www.sb1440.org/Counseling.aspx.

Fong, P. *Assembly Bill 2302,* 2010. Retrieved Sept. 17, 2012, from www.leginfo.ca.gov/pub/09-10/bill/asm/ab_2301-2350/ab_2302_bill_20100929_chaptered.html.

Kisker, C. B., Wagoner, R. L., and Cohen, A. M. *Implementing Statewide Transfer & Articulation Reform: An Analysis of Transfer Associate Degrees in Four States.* Los Angeles: Center for the Study of Community Colleges, 2011.

Kisker, C. B., Cohen, A. M, and Wagoner, A. L. *Reforming Transfer and Articulation in California: Four Statewide Solutions for Creating a More Successful and Seamless Transfer Path to the Baccalaureate.* Los Angeles: Center for the Study of Community Colleges, 2010.

The Legislative Analyst's Office. *Reforming the State's Transfer Process: A Progress Report on Senate Bill 1440.* Sacramento, Calif.: Author, 2012. Retrieved Sept. 17, 2012, from http://lao.ca.gov/laoapp/PubDetails.aspx?id=2631.

Transfer Task Force. *Findings and Recommendations Aimed at Strengthening the Community College Transfer Process.* An interim report to CCC Chancellor Jack Scott, CSU Chancellor Charles Reed, and UC President Mark Yudov. Sacramento, Calif.: Author, 2009.

Padilla, A. Senate Bill 1440. Student Transfer Achievement Reform Act, 2010. Retrieved Sept. 17, 2012, from www.leginfo.ca.gov/pub/09-10/bill/sen/sb_1401-1450/sb_1440_bill_20100929_chaptered.html.

JANE PATTON *served as the president of the Academic Senate for California Community Colleges from 2008 to 2010. She chaired the Intersegmental Curriculum Workgroup during the initial implementation of SB 1440. During the 2010–2011 academic year she became faculty coordinator for the Complete College American grant and served as the faculty coordinator for C-ID.*

MICHELLE PILATI *served as the president of the Academic Senate for California Community Colleges from 2010 to 2012. During the initial implementation of SB 1440 she was vice president of the Academic Senate for California Community Colleges and faculty coordinator for C-ID.*

Presidential leadership contributed to the implementation of New Jersey's transfer articulation legislation.

The Role of Presidential Leadership in Improving New Jersey's Community College Transfer Experience

Casey Maliszewski, Kathleen Crabill, Lawrence Nespoli

For the past 45 years, New Jersey community colleges have helped thousands of students pursue higher education to gain skills, earn college credentials, and better their lives. Today, New Jersey's 19 community colleges enroll over 400,000 students across 70 campuses, fulfilling community colleges' traditional core mission: granting *access* to higher education. Yet while access remains core to our mission and an essential goal, it is no longer a sufficient aim. Our country's economic future depends on our ability to develop an educated, highly skilled workforce. By 2018, nearly two thirds of all American jobs will require a postsecondary certificate or degree (Carnevale, Smith, and Strohl, 2010). If the United States were to proceed with current college graduation rates, our country would not produce enough graduates to fill these new jobs. Such projections make it imperative that institutions of higher education improve the number of students completing a college credential. For their part, community colleges across the country are adopting a refined and recharged mission with *access to success* at its core.

To address this critical mission of college completion and student success, along with the more challenging fiscal climate, New Jersey's community college trustees and presidents agreed to pursue collectively the best and boldest ideas to promote economic sustainability, improve quality, and most significantly, improve student success. Launched in 2010 by the New

Jersey Council of County Colleges and chaired by all 19 community college presidents, the Big Ideas Project consisted of eight work groups with membership from all of the New Jersey community colleges. The groups have tackled work across eight important areas:

1. Transforming Developmental Education
2. Aligning Expectations Between K–12 and Community Colleges
3. Improving Student Success Data
4. Promoting Adjunct Faculty Development
5. Enhancing Joint Purchases
6. Promoting Academic Consortia
7. Building Alternative Learning Systems
8. Using Core Student Learning Outcomes and Common Assessment Tools

Each of these initiatives has made progress in the two years since the Big Ideas Project began. In transforming developmental education, for example, the presidents approved a statewide plan aimed at improving the success of developmental education, and in fall 2012, the state's community colleges convened a first-ever Student Success Summit to engage faculty teams in the implementation of these important recommendations. Another example of significant progress is the presidents' approval of a revised Student Success Model. Based on emerging national trends and developed by the statewide community college Institutional Research Officers, this robust data model is being pilot tested by seven New Jersey community colleges. Finally, after identifying the 10 highest-enrollment community college general education courses in the state and collecting course syllabi for each course, New Jersey is in the process of identifying common student learning outcomes, appropriate teaching methods, and core assessment tools.

In addition to these significant efforts to strengthen student achievement in postsecondary education, one issue critical to college completion and improving student success continues to be the student transfer experience from community colleges to baccalaureate institutions. As Kisker, Wagoner, and Cohen (2011) write, "Improving what is often a complex community college-to-university transfer process, many analysts argue, is key to improve bachelor's degree production" (p. iii). Especially in a time when college tuition has increasingly gotten more expensive, more traditional-aged students are beginning at community colleges, hoping to transfer credits into a four-year college or university. In 2003, students who were less than 22 years old represented 44 percent of the total New Jersey community college enrollment. However, by 2010, this jumped by 7 percentage points to 51 percent (State of New Jersey Higher Education, 2011). And whereas total enrollment across New Jersey community colleges increased by 17 percent between 2006 and 2010, transfer rates from New Jersey community colleges to four-year colleges and universities in New Jersey increased by almost 33 percent. With more students coming to community colleges with the goal of transferring, the issue of ensuring smooth transitions from community colleges to four-year colleges or universities became even more of an imperative. It is New Jersey's dedication to this critical issue that led to the passage of New Jersey's transfer articulation legislation in 2007: Assembly Bill 3968, otherwise known as the "Lampitt Bill."

Pre–Lampitt Bill: Laying the Groundwork

A number of events in New Jersey led to passage of the Lampitt Bill. In 1997, staff and faculty from the 19 community colleges worked together to develop a general education foundation for associate of arts, associate of science, specialized associate, and certificate programs. Since then, New Jersey's community colleges have maintained the development of a statewide process for reviewing and approving general education courses, which is led by the colleges' chief academic officers. Any newly proposed general education courses from any college are reviewed against a common rubric, which is analyzed by the academic officers who work together to examine the course content and student learning outcomes. Courses meeting the standard as an approved general education course are recommended to the presidents for approval. Additionally, in 2007, New Jersey community colleges standardized placement tests and cut scores for remediation. These two efforts supported the development of a common approach to transfer.

Legislative initiatives also contributed to the need for a stronger transfer articulation. New Jersey, as a matter of public policy, has taken the approach of encouraging more students to start at a public community college. One of the policies that facilitated this was the creation of NJ STARS (www.njstars.net) in 2004, a scholarship exclusively for New Jersey students who graduate in the top 15 percent of their high school class that covers the cost of tuition at any of New Jersey's 19 community colleges. This landmark legislation was the first program of its kind in the country to target merit-based scholarships specifically to community college students. NJ STARS II, a scholarship for NJ STARS graduates who transfer to a New Jersey college or university, began in 2006. Another initiative began in 2003 when the legislature started a pilot program, called Tuition Aid Grants (TAGs), for part-time community college students. This program offers eligible students state financial aid and now provides over $10 million in scholarships each year to over 10,000 needy part-time students.

These policies helped elevate the role of community colleges in New Jersey's higher education system. However, given the increasing number of younger students aiming to transfer from community colleges to four-year colleges and universities, these policies would only make sense if community college students could successfully transfer to senior colleges without having to repeat courses. It soon became apparent that there was an alarming gap for transfer students in New Jersey. For example, as Kisker,

Wagoner, and Cohen (2011) report, New Jersey legislators heard stories of students across the state who had to repeat courses upon transferring (p. 9). Policymakers were concerned that the funds that went into supporting students' community college education (including state and county funding, as well as student and family resources) were, in many ways, wasted because the students would take the same courses after transferring. It was clear that something needed to be done to better support students by allowing them to seamlessly transfer and apply community college credits to a senior institution.

The Lampitt Bill

Given the groundwork that had been laid previously, New Jersey State Assemblywoman Pamela Lampitt sponsored Assembly Bill 3968 (New Jersey Legislature, 2006), to help students transfer seamlessly into a baccalaureate institution. The bill, which was passed unanimously, required public New Jersey colleges and universities to enter into a statewide transfer agreement that provided for the full transfer of academic credits from a completed associate of arts or associate of science degree program to a baccalaureate degree program. The bill directed the New Jersey Presidents' Council—which is composed of the presidents of all two- and four-year, public, private, independent, and proprietary institutions in the state—to develop the details of the agreement. According to the bill, the Council was to work in consultation with what was then the New Jersey Commission on Higher Education (in 2012, the Office of the Secretary of Higher Education took over all responsibilities previously held by the Commission on Higher Education) to develop a comprehensive statewide transfer agreement that detailed the policies and procedures that would provide for this full transfer of community college credits to senior institutions.

Prior to the legislation, there were only college-to-college articulation agreements, in which a single senior institution would enter into a transfer agreement with a particular community college. However, to take advantage of these agreements, students had to target a transfer institution early in their college career to ensure they took the appropriate courses specific to that agreement. Once the statewide transfer agreement was implemented, students could choose from a wide range of transfer options. While some of the college-to-college agreements still exist, they are now supplemental to the statewide transfer agreement.

In addition, the Lampitt Bill required four-year universities to annually submit data on the transfer of credits to the Office of Higher Education and required an annual report that includes "an analysis of the effect of the agreement on the transfer process and on the academic success of transfer students at the senior institutions, and an analysis of each participating institution's compliance with the provisions of this act" (New Jersey Legislature, 2006, p. 2). The report, in its current form, shows the percent-

THE ROLE OF PRESIDENTIAL LEADERSHIP   73

age of community college graduates who received half or more of the credits needed for the bachelor's degree when they transferred—both statewide and for individual state colleges and universities.

Finally, the legislation required each of the senior institutions to develop, implement, and publicize an appeals process that enables students to submit a formal request that a college or university reevaluate the transfer and application of credits. If a student believes that a receiving institution did not act appropriately under the statewide transfer agreement, the student files an appeal directly to the receiving college.

To help communicate this agreement to students and their families, the state utilized an existing Web site called NJ Transfer (www.njtransfer.org). Developed previously as a joint initiative of the New Jersey Commission on Higher Education and the New Jersey Presidents' Council, the Web site provides information about transfer articulation and allows students to find course equivalencies, plan their academic program, and evaluate courses. The Web-based transfer tool has significantly helped students prepare for transfer at any point in their community college experience. With the Lampitt Bill and the NJ Transfer program in place, the stage was set for college presidents throughout the state to play the key role in implementing New Jersey's statewide transfer efforts. Their leadership led to the creation of the important details that would ultimately realize the legislation's vision.

The Importance of Presidential Leadership in Facilitating Implementation

The New Jersey Presidents' Council was the implementing body for the transfer legislation. The Council formally adopted the necessary agreements to enact what the legislature demanded: an agreement on the full transfer of the associate degree, the requirement that students have a process to challenge actions that do not honor that full transfer, and the requirement that the results of the legislation be collected and reported annually.

The first requirement was to develop the required statewide transfer agreement, outlining how the colleges would comply with the law's requirements. The statewide transfer agreement was drafted by a core group of presidents and was both simple in its approach—equating an associate degree with 50 percent of the credits required for a bachelor's degree—and direct in its intent, confirming a "corollary principle" that transfer students should not face requirements different from those imposed on native students. Specifically, the agreement stipulated that any "A.A. or A.S. degree from a New Jersey community college will be fully transferable as the first two years of a baccalaureate degree program at New Jersey public four-year institutions" (New Jersey Presidents' Council, 2008, p. 1). Further, the agreement specified that students would, upon their enrollment at the baccalaureate institution, automatically hold junior status. The agreement also noted that any 100- and 200-level courses of equivalent content would be accepted at four-year universities, and recognized the complexity of college curricula, noting that a receiving institution should provide a student with clear direction about those remaining credits that would constitute the second half of the degree. There was significant opportunity for discussion and revision—at both the sector and the Presidents' Council levels—of the agreement before it was completed. Through this deliberative process, presidential leadership statewide provided an unambiguous endorsement of the law's intention.

New Jersey has a designated structure for coordinating statewide transfer issues, the New Jersey Presidents' Council Transfer Committee. The statewide transfer agreement specifically charged the New Jersey Presidents' Council Transfer Committee with the following responsibilities:

- Assessing the effectiveness of the implementation of the Statewide Transfer Agreement, in particular: (a) the rates of achievement of baccalaureate degrees by transfer students, and (b) the actual implementation of the terms of the Statewide Transfer Agreement by participating institutions.
- Recommending to the Presidents' Council any modifications to the statewide transfer agreement or related procedures.
- Hearing appeals from institutions on behalf of students.
- Impaneling ad hoc subcommittees, if and when necessary, to research and make recommendations in regard to specific issues related to transfer.

Membership on the Transfer Committee consists of five senior college representatives, five community college representatives, one proprietary school representative, and one representative from the Office of the Secretary of Higher Education.

Beyond the initial implementation efforts, the Presidents' Council charged its Transfer Committee with continuing to work on the spirit of the legislation, eliminating barriers to successful transfer. To that end, the committee began by conducting regional summits for professional staff and faculty involved in transfer to explore the issues that were most likely to thwart the straightforward implementation of the statewide transfer agreement. Supported by the Presidents' Council, these summits identified specific disciplines or programs that had more levels of complication: specific course sequences, differing prerequisites, complicated experiential or externship requirements, and great variations among institutions either at the associate degree or baccalaureate level. What emerged was a call for additional work in facilitating transfer in popular majors. This work will be modeled on statewide articulation agreements developed in other states and will provide students and their families with a more direct and less confusing path to accomplishing their educational goals without limiting institutional autonomy or faculty creativity. Thus, the next effort will be to build a professional team from all sectors of higher education to develop transfer pathways in three areas identified as high interest for students and high challenge in transfer: psychology, business, and education.

The Transfer Committee also considers the formal reports from each of the senior public institutions each year, and has identified several challenges that cross institutional lines. One key challenge is the number of students whose associate degree is not presented to the receiving institution. This has raised logistical challenges that the Transfer Committee is addressing, including more effective and efficient ways of producing and transmitting transcript data between institutions, along with potential improvements to the statewide data system. It has also identified ways in which institutions can better communicate with students about the importance of providing accurate, timely information throughout the transfer process.

The Presidents' Council Transfer Committee existed prior to the implementation of the Lampitt legislation, but the legislation provided a powerful guide for the committee. The law provided the opportunity for New Jersey's presidents to assert, formally, their support for the importance of the transfer function and, through the statewide transfer agreement, their confidence in the associate degree.

In looking at New Jersey's experience implementing the Lampitt Bill, some key lessons emerge. First, although presidential leadership at the community college level played an integral role in creating and implementing the transfer articulation policy, presidential leadership at the senior institutions also had a profound influence. In New Jersey's case, a president from a state university took a leadership role in bridging the two groups. Without this individual's guidance and insight, it may have been more difficult to get the senior colleges on board with the vision of the Lampitt Bill. Second, although the policy's scope included only public institutions, the legislation has also had an impact on private institutions throughout the state. Although private colleges are not subject to the legislation, many private institutions—not wanting to miss out on attracting transfer students—have entered into their own transfer agreements with community colleges. Therefore, the bill provided some leverage with which to incentivize private colleges' participation in helping to improve the transfer process. In some cases, these private colleges have gone above and beyond what the legislation requires, allowing students to transfer up to 75 or 90 percent of the credits necessary for a bachelor's degree, compared to the 50 percent guaranteed by the Lampitt Bill. Finally, although the legislation has had a profound impact on improving the transfer experience, it requires constant effort to ensure that its vision is being carried out. This process requires community college leaders to be vigilant in monitoring the transfer processes to ensure the policies are upheld with fidelity.

Moving Forward: What Is Next for New Jersey's Transfer Experience?

New Jersey has made much progress in improving statewide transfer policies and practices since the passage of the Lampitt Bill. But as is usually the case with bold initiatives, continued energy and resources are needed to keep things moving in the right direction after the initial burst of activity subsides. As Kisker, Wagoner, and Cohen (2011) note in their analysis of transfer reform in several key states:

> We were struck by the power of personality in enacting large-scale organizational change. Yet individuals do not develop transfer associate degrees on their own; to be effective in implementing systemic transform reforms, they must work through a clear and ongoing organizational structure. (p. 12)

Such has surely been the case in New Jersey as strong personalities—both in the legislature and among the college presidents—led to the enactment of the Lampitt Bill and the subsequent approval of the statewide transfer agreement by the New Jersey Presidents' Council. Since then, an effective structure has emerged through the work of the Transfer Committee, and the various student challenges that cause institutions to re-think the application of policy under the requirements of the statewide transfer agreement. This structure must be supported by clear and consistent information and must include what is expected of the students, of the sending institutions, and of the receiving institutions. It should contain clear guidance for students about when and where a final transcript must be sent. There may be some benefit in the community college sector of standardizing parts of the transcript to facilitate clear communication. There is certainly benefit in fully implementing an electronic transcript system to ensure timely delivery of important student information. All of these issues are under review by the Transfer Committee in an effort to continue to improve this process and to ensure full compliance with the spirit of the legislation. New Jersey's experience confirms that an organizational structure and support system, coupled with the ongoing attention of the higher education leadership, can help to maintain momentum in transfer reform.

What are New Jersey's next steps in reenergizing its transfer reform agenda? First, New Jersey community college presidents are recommitting to the cause and are taking this recommitment to their four-year colleagues on the Transfer Committee. The bottom line is that some modest resources are needed to ensure continuity in these efforts. However, it is a delicate process. For all of the obvious reasons, there has to be joint ownership of transfer activities by both community colleges and senior colleges throughout the state. There seems to be an emerging consensus among the Presidents' Council Transfer Committee on the first priorities for reenergizing the statewide transfer reform agenda.

Strengthening Data Collection. It is important to strengthen the annual collection of transfer data required by the Lampitt Bill so that efforts are more evidence-based in the future. New Jersey needs to take a closer look at the community college graduates who are not accepted with full junior status when they transfer so that stakeholders can better understand what happened and why. The following questions need to be answered about these students: What was their community college major? What was their senior college major? What community college did they transfer from? What senior college did they transfer to?

Identifying Early-Major Pathways. The evidence is clear from other states that transfer sequences in select disciplines are important tools for improving statewide transfer practices. Thus far, education, business, and psychology have been identified as the disciplines that will be first to build early-major pathways in New Jersey.

Involving Faculty. Another priority is convening regular meetings of discipline-based faculty work groups to develop the major-to-major transfer pathways as well as provide overall leadership on statewide transfer reform efforts. When all is said and done, faculty leadership and involvement matters most in achieving successful transfer results for community college students.

There is no doubt that New Jersey has made great strides in improving the community college transfer experience. Thanks to strong state transfer legislation and the leadership of New Jersey's college presidents, students throughout the state can be guaranteed a smoother transfer from community colleges to baccalaureate-granting institutions. While progress still needs to be made to address some specific remaining challenges, New Jersey will continue to move forward to improve transfer processes and, as a result, improve college completion.

References

Carnevale, A., Smith, N., and Strohl, J. *Help Wanted: Projections of Jobs and Education Requirements*. Washington, D.C.: Georgetown University, Center on Education and the Workforce, 2010. Retrieved July 1, 2012, from www9.georgetown.edu/grad/gppi/hpi/cew/pdfs/HelpWanted.FullReport.pdf.

Kisker, C., Wagoner, R., and Cohen, A. *Implementing Statewide Transfer & Articulation Reform: An Analysis of Transfer Associate Degrees in Four States*. Los Angeles: Center for the Study of Community Colleges, 2011.

New Jersey Legislature. *Assembly Bill 3968, Chapter 175*. Trenton, N.J.: Author, 2006. Retrieved September 20, 2012, from www.njleg.state.nj.us/2006/Bills/PL07/175_.PDF.

New Jersey Presidents' Council. *Comprehensive Statewide Transfer Agreement*. Trenton, N.J.: Author, 2008. Retrieved June 1, 2012, from www.nj.gov/highereducation/PDFs/XferAgreementOct08.pdf.

State of New Jersey Higher Education. *Frequently Requested Statistical Tables*. Trenton, N.J.: Author, 2011. Retrieved June 4, 2012, from www.state.nj.us/highereducation/statistics/index.html.

CASEY MALISZEWSKI *is a program associate with Achieve and a former research assistant with the New Jersey Council of County Colleges.*

KATHLEEN CRABILL *is president of Raritan Valley Community College and is co-chair of the Transfer Committee of the New Jersey Presidents' Council.*

LAWRENCE NESPOLI *is president of the New Jersey Council of County Colleges.*

8

This chapter provides an overview of the transfer model in Arizona, including the Arizona General Education Curriculum (AGEC), transfer associate degrees, and a shared course numbering system. It highlights the importance of collaborations between the community colleges and universities, and among public institutions of higher education and the K–12 system.

Developing a Culture of Transfer and Student Success in Arizona

Maria Harper-Marinick, Jeanne Swarthout

Student success in transfer from a community college to a university is dependent on several key characteristics of any articulation and transfer system: structure, policies and processes, and the accessibility of the system design. The public institutions of higher education in Arizona have designed and implemented a transfer and articulation system with these key characteristics made central.

Infrastructure of Arizona's Transfer Model

Arizona's structure for implementing, maintaining, and improving the transfer process has evolved over time in response to legislative mandates and on-the-ground determinations of what is necessary in order to develop and improve the state's culture of transfer and student success. The following sections detail the main components of Arizona's transfer infrastructure.

Academic Program Articulation Steering Committee. The Academic Program Articulation Steering Committee (APASC) was established in 1983 by the Joint Conference Committee of the Arizona State Board of Regents (ABOR) and the State Board of Directors for Community Colleges in Arizona and charged with oversight of transfer articulation for the public community colleges and universities. APASC is the coordinating body of the statewide articulation and transfer system. It recommends institutional policy changes and provides oversight of curricular alignment among

Arizona's public post-secondary educational institutions. APASC is overseen by the Joint Council of Presidents (JCP), which includes the chief executive officers of the 10 community college districts and the three universities, as well as the president of ABOR. APASC's organizational structure provides for representation of faculty and administrators from Arizona's public and tribal community colleges and universities, and its membership is comprised of senior academic leaders from the three state universities, ABOR, and representatives from both urban and rural community colleges. APASC is co-chaired by a university and a community college representative on a rotating basis, and its work is supported by the APASC executive director and staff members who coordinate statewide transfer efforts in the areas of data collection and reporting, technology, marketing, and articulation facilitation. The state universities, community college districts, and tribal colleges jointly fund APASC.

APASC oversees the work of the following task forces and subcommittees that perform the key functions on behalf of the organization: Institutional Articulation Facilitators, Academic Affairs Articulation Task Force, Admissions and Records Articulation Task Force, Discipline Articulation Task Forces, Data and Evaluation subcommittee, Marketing and Communications subcommittee, Technology subcommittee, and the Consortium for Transfer and Alignment. Two of these groups are detailed in the following paragraphs.

Discipline Articulation Task Forces. Articulation Task Forces (ATFs) are discipline-specific faculty groups that play a critical role in ensuring the articulation of courses and programs. Discipline-specific ATFs are organized by subject matter and concentrate on curriculum issues, how courses taught at Arizona community colleges and public universities should transfer, and how to attain the best lower-division preparation for each specific discipline. Each community college or university that offers courses in a given area is eligible for membership in the respective ATF. ATFs make recommendations to confirm current baccalaureate degrees and place new degrees in pathways that articulate with the two-year transfer degrees; increase commonality among lower-division requirements of majors shared by two or more institutions; maintain at least six credits of lower-division coursework common to the shared university majors; identify the appropriate level for new courses according to APASC's Criteria for Upper- and Lower-Division Courses; and affirm the appropriate general education track for each major's lower-division preparation.

APASC Consortium for Transfer and Alignment. The APASC Consortium for Transfer and Alignment (ACTA) was formed to respond to state and national needs for more individuals to successfully complete a college education and enter the workforce, and to foster collaboration along the P-20 continuum for improved student achievement. With greater emphasis placed on student success and completion, APASC quickly recognized the need to include K–12 educators in its transfer and articulation work. By creating ACTA, APASC has provided a forum for meaningful conversations and curricular alignment work between K–12 and higher education that will strengthen the connections between the systems, promote college and career readiness, provide earlier opportunities for students to experience college success, increase access to higher education, and make the transitions from one system to the next more transparent. ACTA members include the chief academic officers from each of the public and tribal postsecondary institutions, two urban and two rural high school superintendents, two Joint Technical Education District (JTED) superintendents representing rural and urban areas, a member of the Arizona Department of Education, a member of the Governor's office, and community representatives.

ACTA's goals include developing formal ties with the K–12 system and the Arizona Department of Education as key partners in transfer and articulation; enhancing curricular alignment between the secondary and postsecondary institutions; developing and implementing marketing and advertising strategies to ensure that transfer information is disseminated to multiple stakeholders in an effective, efficient, and timely manner; and improving student support systems. While ACTA is not yet a mature organization, it has identified a number of immediate tasks including the evaluation of a unified student transcript system for the state, dissemination of ACTA's work throughout the K–12 system, and enhanced awareness of pathway and transfer options among K–12 advisors.

APASC, as well as its many task forces and subcommittees, is responsible for the state's common general education curriculum, as well as transfer associate degrees and other premajor transfer pathways. These are detailed in the following section.

The Arizona General Education Curriculum (AGEC) and Transfer Associate Degrees

In 1996, the Arizona Legislature (ARS 15-1824) directed the state's community college districts and universities to

> cooperate in operating a statewide articulation and transfer system, including the process for transfer of lower-division general education credits, general elective credits and curriculum requirements for approved majors, to facilitate the transfer of community college students to Arizona public universities without a loss of credit toward a baccalaureate degree and to ensure that the postsecondary education needs of students statewide are met without unnecessary duplication of programs.

In response to this legislative directive, ABOR and the State Board of Directors for Community Colleges of Arizona established a Transfer Articulation Task Force (TATF) to develop a model that would bolster Arizona's articulation system and improve student access to the state university system. The TATF designed a transfer model to create clear and secure transfer pathways for community college students. These pathways are designed to allow students to maximize their academic experience at the community colleges, to incorporate community college credits or degrees efficiently into university graduation requirements, and to complete baccalaureate degrees based on a minimum number of required credits. APASC was charged with the implementation and monitoring of this model.

Arizona's transfer system provides general, specific, and exceptional pathways for transfer. It is based on the Arizona General Education Curriculum (AGEC), which provides a general education core for four transfer associate degrees. Including the AGEC, community college students may transfer up to one half of the baccalaureate degree requirements plus one course, or up to 64 units.

Arizona General Education Curriculum (AGEC). The AGEC provides a general education core for the four transfer associate degrees. It is composed of 35 to 38 credits and constitutes over half of the unit requirements for transfer associate degrees. Community college students who complete the AGEC satisfy all lower division general education requirements at the three state universities.

A study of Arizona's transfer system conducted by Hezel Associates in 2007 found a direct correlation between the completion of the AGEC prior to transfer and successful completion of a baccalaureate degree after transfer. All of Arizona's public colleges and universities have made significant efforts to promote completion of the AGEC, which has resulted in a sharp increase in the number of AGECs awarded by community colleges: 8,250 in 2011. This number is triple the number of completions in 2002 (APASC, 2011).

Transfer Degrees. Most students planning university transfer are best served by completing an associate's degree at a community college. There are four primary statewide degrees: associate in art, associate in business, associate in science, and associate in arts in elementary education. Students who participate in these degree programs at the community college level are assured a seamless transfer to a public university without loss of credits. The number of students transferring to the universities with a transfer associate degree (which have the AGEC embedded) has doubled since 2004 (APASC, 2011).

Maricopa to ASU Pathways Program. In 2009, the Maricopa Community College District and Arizona State University (ASU) developed an innovative transfer program designed to increase the number of students who complete a community college degree and transfer to the university for completion of a bachelor's degree in the most efficient and cost-effective manner. The Maricopa to ASU Pathways Program (MAPP) was designed for students who want to start at the community college and plan to complete a bachelor's degree at ASU. The MAPPs build on the elements of transfer degrees that work well, including completion of the AGEC, but provide a prescriptive pathway of clear and specific coursework within a major. This ensures that every course on a MAPP transfers and applies to an ASU degree with no loss of credit.

MAPP is based on five principles supported by research and effective practices: excellent academic preparation, increased financial support, joint training for student advisors, data sharing to monitor progress, and an electronic transcript system. Students on a MAPP follow a prescribed sequence of coursework at any of the Maricopa Community Colleges, earn the appropriate AGEC, complete the lower-division course requirements for an ASU major, and are guaranteed admission to the degree program at ASU. Benefits for the students include guaranteed admission to ASU degree programs, well-defined pathways that ensure that all the courses transfer and apply to the selected ASU degree, eligibility for participation in the ASU Tuition Commitment program, access to merit scholarships, and transfer support and preenrollment services by ASU transfer staff who spend time at the community college campuses. In 2012, there were 125 MAPPs available to students. Pathways were initially developed for the most popular degrees, but the goal of the partnership is to have most degrees at ASU on a MAPP. The response from students has been very positive. MAPP enrollments almost doubled in a mere 12 months, from 4,982 at the conclusion of the 2010–2011 academic year to 8,125 as of fall 2012.

Transfer Admission Guarantees. A variation on the MAPP model, Transfer Admission Guarantees (TAGs) have worked effectively in small, rural community colleges. For example, at Northland Pioneer College (NPC), located in an isolated, rural area of Arizona, it is not feasible to offer the diversity of degrees and certificates available in a metropolitan area. Thus, beginning in 2009, ASU and NPC began to develop TAGs that are similar to MAPPs but tailored to a different educational environment. NPC currently has 14 TAG agreements with ASU. These agreements allow NPC students to complete more or all of their coursework with ASU without leaving their home communities. The TAG agreements between NPC and ASU give participating students the opportunity to transfer up to 75 lower-division, specified courses to the university. The remaining upper-division ASU courses can be taken online from the student's community college or on-site at ASU. Additionally, TAGs guarantee admission to ASU and specific programs upon completion of the required coursework. Currently, a number of NPC students who completed their associate of applied science in nursing are enrolled at ASU through a TAG agreement; these students will complete their BSN efficiently, conserve financial resources, and remain in their communities where they serve a vital role.

Shared Course Numbering System

In 2009, new legislation (Senate Bill 1186, codified in ARS 15-1824) required Arizona's public universities and community colleges to develop and implement a shared course numbering system, which identifies courses that transfer from community colleges to the universities and apply toward a baccalaureate degree. Some legislators believed that a shared course numbering system would create easier, seamless, and more transparent pathways from community colleges to universities.

Thus, the JCP established a Shared Numbering Steering Committee (SC) to oversee its development in response to SB 1186. The SC included the executive vice chancellors and provosts from the Maricopa and Pima community college districts, a representative from ABOR, the APASC co-chairs, and a business analyst. In addition, a statewide Shared Numbering System Committee (SNSC), consisting of representatives from all 10 Arizona community college districts and the three universities, was established under the direction of the SC to review options, analyze costs, recommend a preferred approach, and begin planning for the implementation of the selected system. The SC and SNSC were responsible for the eventual implementation of the system and for engaging faculty and staff in conversations as necessary. APASC was asked to assume the monitoring of the system after implementation.

The SNSC considered several models for common course numbering that had been implemented in other states, and decided on one that could be adopted at a low cost to the institutions and cause the least disruption to the transfer model already in place. In the adopted model, community college and university courses with established equivalencies are assigned a shared unique number (SUN), very distinctive from any of the existing institutional numbering systems. A SUN number is comprised of a unique three-letter prefix and four-digit course number. For example, MAT 1187 is the SUN for precalculus and MAT 2220 is the SUN for calculus I. MAT was selected as the SUN prefix for these courses because it was the most commonly used prefix for mathematics among the institutions. The first digit of the four-digit SUN indicates whether the course is a first-year course (1 for precalculus) or a second-year course (2 for calculus I); the last three digits of the SUN number are the most commonly used numbers for the two courses among the institutions. The SUN system is now a bank of identifiable common courses that are mapped to each institution's existing courses. The institution's own prefixes and numbers do not change and continue to be used internally. However, catalogs, transcripts, Web sites/databases, and degree audit programs must also reflect the SUN.

The implementation of Arizona's shared course numbering system has gone well. All community colleges and universities have included the SUN numbering icon in all course catalogs, databases, and degree audit systems; all place links to the SUN Web site (www.azsunsystem.com) on their Web sites, especially student portals, transfer program pages, and news or blog sections; and all promote SUN on social media profiles.

The Importance of Institutional Collaborations in Improving Transfer

Several formal collaborations support Arizona's transfer model, and in particular the state's MAPPs and TAGs. Perhaps most important, Getting AHEAD: Access to Higher Education and Degrees, is a comprehensive and collaborative initiative that engages Arizona's universities, community colleges, K–12 sector, business community, and legislative and executive branches of government in increasing the educational attainment of Arizonans by making degrees more accessible and affordable and by enabling more residents to obtain a college degree or certificate. The initiative is made possible through a grant from the Lumina Foundation. Major objectives being pursued through this initiative include expanding partnerships between the universities and the community colleges; implementing a student-centered system that improves advising and career planning; increasing institutional efficiencies and developing a new higher education financing model; improving the coordination and governance of public postsecondary institutions; and implementing a communication and public engagement program. The goals of Getting AHEAD closely align with the work being done through APASC and ACTA to ensure that students are better prepared for postsecondary work and careers.

The Getting AHEAD project provided the impetus for MAPPs and TAGs, as well as other new collaborations between Arizona's community colleges and the public universities. These partnerships provide students with greater access to affordable higher education programs and incentives for completing degrees and certificates. Collaborations include joint admissions where students start at the community college and are simultaneously admitted to the university with full student privileges; bachelor's degree pathways from the community colleges into the universities (over 500 MAPPs and TAGs have been developed between the 10 community college districts and the three universities); guaranteed admissions into specific programs at the universities; tuition incentives and savings; student merit scholarships; dedicated transfer advisors; university courses and programs offered at community college campuses that allow students to complete baccalaureate degrees in their hometowns; and the tracking of student performance.

Technology Tools for Transfer

In addition to the programs described earlier, Arizona has developed several technology tools to assist students, faculty, administrators, and statewide transfer personnel in implementing and maintaining the state's transfer system.

AZTransfer.com. AZTransfer.com is Arizona's Web site for transfer. This site is designed for use by students who intend to transfer within

Arizona's public institutions of higher education and by faculty, advisors, and other staff who assist them. One of the most significant components of the site is a portal for high school students that contains college planning and transfer tools such as a dual enrollment database and a link to KnowHow2Go, the portal that helps students plan the steps needed to apply to and attend college; access to the Exam Equivalency Guide; access to a Transfer Options page containing various degree pathways; and a link to the Arizona Career Information System (AzCIS).

Education and Career Action Plans. APASC staff are also collaborating with the Arizona Department of Education to provide data and information that supports the Education and Career Action Plans system (ECAP). Beginning with the class of 2013, all students in grades 9 through 12 at Arizona public schools will be required to complete an individualized plan for their academic and career goals through ECAP. AGEC courses from every community college have been loaded into the ECAP high school portal, giving high school students access to postsecondary planning information within a Web site they are already using.

Arizona State System for Information on Student Transfer. Arizona State System for Information on Student Transfer (ASSIST) provides the data to monitor transfer patterns and information on student success. The database holds records for nearly 2.5 million current and former students who have taken over 26 million courses. For example, statewide and institutional transfer rates for new-to-higher education student cohorts are tracked through ASSIST. In 2012–2013, ASSIST staff will work in collaboration with the Arizona Department of Education to provide key data elements for the State Longitudinal Database System that will track students along the P-20 and workforce continuum.

Other transfer tools that serve statewide articulation and transfer projects include the AGECWeb, Major Guides, the Course Equivalency Guide (CEG), the Arizona Course Equivalency Tracking System (ACETS), the Academic Curriculum Review and Evaluation System (ACRES), and the ATF Chatlines. AGECWeb allows the community colleges to maintain their lists of AGEC courses, and allows students to view the most up-to-date information on these courses. For students who have selected a major but not a university, the Major Guides provide a list of recommended lower-division courses at the student's community college. The CEG is a statewide electronic database that provides detailed information on how community college courses transfer to the three public universities. Users can search for course equivalency by subject, institution, and course number. ACETS is the electronic process by which community and tribal colleges submit their courses to the universities for evaluation for equivalencies. Evaluated courses then are included in the CEG. ACRES is a curriculum routing system developed as a companion tool to ACETS; it is an electronic means for creating, routing, evaluating, and approving new courses, course modifications, and course deletions. The ATF Chatlines is a comprehensive resource that allows both institutional and statewide staff to maintain membership databases, curricular degrees and pathways, meeting reports, and the master statewide calendar. It also has features for submitting action items, useful links to portal pages, and help with documentation.

Lessons Learned

Developing a culture of transfer and student success will always be a work in progress. Arizona's highly successful transfer model has resulted from certain key characteristics: collaboration, communication, institutional commitment and will, and very hard work on the part of all. Beyond the general keys to success, there are some very specific lessons learned in the maturing of the Arizona transfer and articulation system.

First, the value of designing and using very efficient communications systems and processes became evident early in the work of APASC. Discipline-specific ATF chairs leading course content meetings needed assistance and training to understand their role, as well as their responsibilities in maintaining CEG sites and communicating issues with APASC. So ATF chair training was developed and placed on the APASC Web site. Similarly, the need to facilitate communication among the various subcommittees whose members are statewide, with participants in ACTA, and with various individuals responsible for transfer at the individual institutions drove the development of a variety of tools to ensure that transfer and articulation systems are readily available, understood, and efficiently used.

Second, prospective students need to know about the transfer tools and pathways in order to think into the future and plan their college education. Effective marketing of transfer tools to students is key to increasing awareness of all the opportunities available to them, facilitating transfer, and consequently improving college-going rates. If students don't know these tools are available, how to use them, or where to find them, all the collaboration and hard work of developing the pathways is for naught.

Finally, an early lesson learned was that when you think you have thought of everything, you haven't. This lesson is primarily a function of the innovation and change inherent in articulation between the community colleges and universities. What was a good articulation plan a few years ago can be markedly improved today; systems and processes must accommodate these innovations quickly and effectively.

Processes for managing the transfer and articulation work of APASC needed to be developed, changed, and redesigned as the higher education environment transformed itself. Some of the questions that required thoughtful development as situations changed included:

- How do you create new discipline-specific ATFs, and how many institutions are required for a new ATF?

- Under what conditions should an ATF be dissolved, and who should make that decision?
- What is the process for mediating an ATF dispute between members regarding course content, delivery method, or assessment?
- What are the timelines acceptable to all institutions regarding catalog preparation when changes to an AGEC, CEG, or SUN course are needed?

More broadly, after decades of relying on a very small staff and the two co-chairs who volunteered their time to keep APASC working as intended, we had to ask ourselves: When does the transfer system, after years of improvement, require the daily attention of more than two voluntary co-chairs with demanding day jobs? We decided the time had come to restructure the organization, and APASC established an executive committee that included the two co-chairs plus two additional members, one representing community colleges and one representing ABOR. It also created a new position, the executive director, and modified a business analyst position into a director of marketing and communication. Finally, APASC hired a new part-time administrative assistant and redesigned the subcommittees, clarifying roles and responsibilities for all of the groups associated with APASC. These changes have helped APASC stay optimally organized for the challenges Arizona's transfer model will face in the future.

Challenges Ahead

Most of the challenges ahead are clear to APASC: maintenance of the high level of collegiality and professionalism; creation and incorporation of yet more ways to promote efficient transfer; carefully tracking transfer student success and disseminating data to stakeholders in a timely manner; and keeping student transfer and success at the center of the effort.

Some of the specific challenges ahead for Arizona's transfer system, and thus for APASC, are the direct result of an environment of increased innovation and collaboration across the state. For example, there is a new need to define a process for multidisciplinary and interdisciplinary AFTs as new fields emerge and institutions combine and reinvent degree programs.

Another challenge for APASC is decreasing institutional costs of participation in the transfer system. As institutions have been affected by diminishing revenues, it has become a high priority to maintain collaboration, participation, and professionalism through distance technology including video meetings, conference calls, and established satellite locations throughout the state. While working to keep costs of participation low may seem an insignificant challenge, it is actually one of the more important ones APASC faces; if frequent communication between partners in transfer diminishes, the transfer system will be less effective for students.

All education providers in Arizona face the challenge of assisting in the development and implementation of a K–20 data-tracking system aimed at increasing student success. Appropriately, APASC is seen as an ideal partner to help design this model data-tracking system that follows students from entry into kindergarten until individuals leave the system either through terminal higher education degrees, direct employment, or attrition.

Another challenge is related to the continuing involvement of two key groups: students and faculty. Frequent focus groups with students assisted greatly in developing, implementing, and refining the Arizona transfer system, and keeping student perspectives at the heart of further changes will be necessary. The second group consists of community college and university faculty who commit content expertise year after year. Without this voluntary commitment, no transfer system will be effective. Faculty members see great value in providing seamless transfer among community colleges and universities, but their ongoing contributions are key to maintaining a successful transfer model, which will necessarily look very different in five years.

Concluding Thoughts

"The Arizona transfer system appears to be working well and is functioning as a tool and system exactly as intended. Through the system students are able to complete their degrees with nearly one semester FTE less coursework than was the case five years ago" (Hezel Associates, 2007, p. 116). While initiated by legislative statute, the success of Arizona's statewide transfer model is due to the level of collaboration and collegiality among the state's public universities, community colleges, and tribal colleges. The roadblocks to seamless transfer and student success—of which there are many—are most often overcome through a series of discussions with the endpoint of mutual understanding and agreement. The infrastructure of Arizona's transfer system has fostered these collaborations, and they are integral to its ongoing support and improvement.

References

Academic Program Articulation Steering Committee. *Articulation, Transfer, and Shared Course Numbering for Arizona Public Postsecondary Education 2011*. Report submitted to the Joint Legislative Budget Committee. Phoenix, Ariz.: Author, 2011. Retrieved Jan. 2, 2013, from www.apascaz.org/resources/JLBC2011Report.pdf.

Hezel Associates. *Evaluation of Arizona's Transfer Articulation System*. Syracuse, N.Y.: Author, 2007. Retrieved Mar. 15, 2012, from www.hezelassociates.com/resources/46-evaluation-of-arizonas-transfer-articulation-system.

MARIA HARPER-MARINICK *is executive vice chancellor and provost for the Maricopa Community College District.*

JEANNE SWARTHOUT *is president of Northland Pioneer College.*

This chapter synthesizes information from the volume; suggests a state-level model organizational structure for implementing transfer associate degrees; describes the interests and values of the major constituencies in systemic transfer reforms; and offers a view to the future, including potential areas of concern.

Putting the Pieces Together and Asking the Hard Questions: Transfer Associate Degrees in Perspective

Richard L. Wagoner, Carrie B. Kisker

The previous six chapters have focused on particular aspects of the processes involved in implementing transfer associate degrees in various states. In this chapter, we synthesize that information by presenting an ideal state-level organizational model for implementing these degrees and describing the various constituencies involved in the process and their motivating interests and values (which, as seen in the previous chapters, may not always be aligned), as well as the types of negotiation and compromise needed to successfully honor these perspectives. Finally, we offer a view to the future and ask some hard questions regarding the future of transfer associate degrees.

While drawing on ideas from the chapters in this volume, this chapter achieves its synthesis of material by focusing on an independent research project we conducted in 2011, which became the basis for the volume overall (Kisker, Wagoner, and Cohen, 2011). As noted in Chapter One, this study consisted of case studies conducted in four states: Arizona, New Jersey, Ohio, and Washington. The project examined the political processes, actors, and associations involved in implementing transfer associate degrees, employing within-state and cross-case analyses to identify strategies and processes that were necessary and effective in their implementation. The case studies involved site visits, analysis of relevant documents, as well as roughly 60 in-depth qualitative interviews with policymakers, system leaders, college presidents and key administrators, faculty, and others involved in implementing these initiatives. Interview questions focused on the formal and informal processes used to develop, implement, and maintain transfer associate degrees, including: which groups were instrumental and in what order they were employed, whether legislation was necessary to compel implementation, how faculty and institutional autonomy were addressed, as well as other areas that reach beyond the limits of this chapter. Interviews took place in person or over the telephone, and were transcribed verbatim prior to inductive coding and analysis.

Ideal State-Level Organizational Structure

As all of the challenges and successes documented earlier in this volume have implied, in order to achieve any level of success implementing transfer associate degrees it is essential to create a clear, ongoing organizational structure to support those efforts. In our original study we were struck by the fact that the power of personality alone was not enough to enact lasting change. We found—and the contributors to this volume have demonstrated—that to be effective in implementing systemic transfer reforms, states must implement organizational structures that assign to each group the tasks to which they are best equipped to carry out. (For example, as Chapters Five and Six in this volume argue, faculty committees must be responsible for all curricular modifications and related decisions.) Figure 9.1

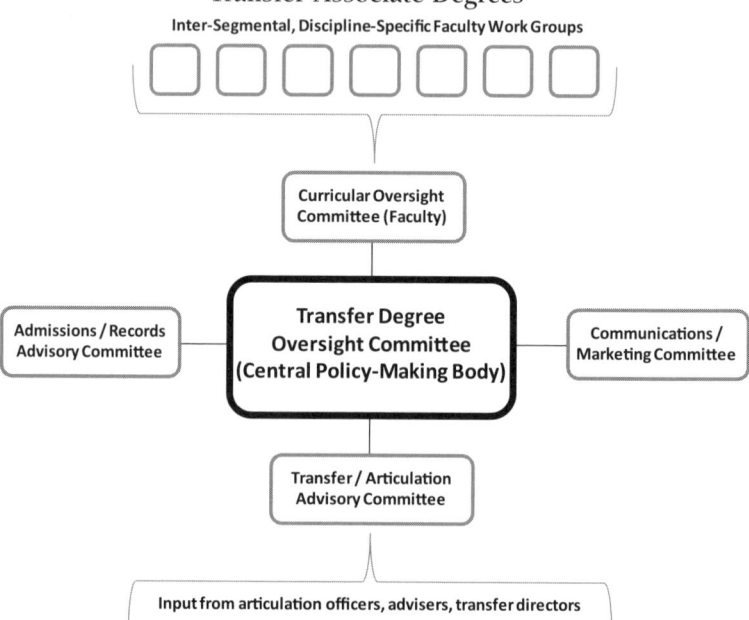

Figure 9.1. Model Organizational Structure for Implementing Transfer Associate Degrees

illustrates a model structure for creating transfer associate degrees, dealing with policy and administrative issues as they arise, and ensuring awareness, buy-in, and compliance among members of the higher education community.

This model organizational structure, some version of which is in place in six states highlighted in this volume, is not hierarchical in form or function. Rather, it allows statewide policy to radiate out from a central policy-making and oversight body; model transfer pathways to emerge from a faculty-led curricular oversight committee; and newly developed policies and programs to be enforced by presidents, provosts, deans, department chairs, and others at the individual district or campus levels. As the previous chapters have made clear, open and ongoing communication is key; therefore, this model ensures communication among all groups and provides venues for identifying and resolving problems related to policy, curriculum, articulation, admissions, and other aspects of the transfer process. Most notably, this structure works well because it assigns responsibility for each aspect of the transfer degree implementation process to the group that is best suited to manage it. The following sections describe the individual committees suggested by the model.

Transfer Degree Oversight Committee. Composed of high-level administrators and faculty leaders who have the authority to enforce policy at the system or campus levels, this group is charged with resolving statewide policy issues. California's SB 1440 Implementation Committee (see Chapter Six) is a good example of a model transfer degree oversight committee. A university administrator described Ohio's version of this body: "The oversight committee is very much representative of people from ... four-year and two-year community colleges that are at significant levels, like academic vice presidents for academic affairs. Key individuals who really have the ability not only to bring resources to the table, but also to impact what's going to happen on their campus."

The transfer degree oversight committee also coordinates and oversees subcommittees dealing with the various administrative aspects of implementation, and may provide staff support to curricular oversight and/or faculty disciplinary work groups. This committee is especially critical to ensure awareness, buy-in, and compliance at the district and campus levels by working closely with presidents, provosts, and vice presidents. As a former Arizona community college administrator made clear, "If you don't have an enforcer, you don't have anything!"

Finally, this committee is the primary body interacting with legislators and other interested parties. A Washington community college administrator explained why this role is so important: "I would try to set up [this committee] in an intermediary position, so that if a hot question got asked to one of the state agencies or a legislator or something, that there was a well-known way to deal with that rather than having it turn into a mallet hitting a gnat ... Say, 'Send something to us because we can probably sort it out in a sensible way without wasting the valuable time of you [policymakers].'"

Curricular Oversight and Faculty Disciplinary Committees. Data from our study, as well as Chapters Five and Six in this volume, stress that faculty must be, as an Ohio university administrator argued, "at the heart of" all curricular matters related to transfer. A Washington university administrator explained further:

> What will we [accept as a common lower-division curriculum] that everyone across the board can agree to? Those kinds of conversations simply cannot be had by people who don't know the curriculum well enough to know the details of those kinds of classes. So it's tremendously important that the faculty get involved. Besides which, the buy-in is so much bigger when the faculty are involved. Administrators can say yes and bless it and do all that sort of thing, but coming down to the operationalizing (sic) of it, it helps to have people on the ground who are familiar with it, who feel like they've had a hand in it and really get it and understand it and can sell it across campus.

Thus, the curricular oversight committee in our model is comprised of two- and four-year faculty leaders in various disciplines, and is charged with resolving curricular issues and developing transfer pathways at a statewide level. The curricular oversight committee also ensures awareness, buy-in, and degree alignment at the district and campus levels by working closely with deans, department chairs, and program directors. Further, it collects and responds to feedback from local academic senates, departments, and curriculum committees.

Perhaps most important, the curricular oversight committee convenes intersegmental, discipline-based faculty work groups (for example, Articulation Task Forces in Arizona) and assists in identifying common, high-quality, lower-division transfer pathways in majors or areas of emphasis that can be implemented statewide. As an Arizona community college professor argued, discipline-based faculty work groups are critical to the successful implementation of transfer associate degrees:

> The decisions have to be made in those little kingdoms. Because ... you've really got to get the buy-in from the people granting the degree, and really the people who sign off on the degree are the faculty members. ... And there needs to be a vehicle where the university faculty actually meet the community college faculty and say, "Oh, I hear what you are saying. Yeah, you are teaching the same thing. Yeah, you're using the same textbook I'm using," and for the community college faculty member to find out where the university folks are headed, and that's what the [faculty disciplinary committee] does. It allows for the communication to occur and allows for progress in the right direction together.

Interviewees in our 2011 study spoke at length about the types of faculty that should be recruited for intersegmental disciplinary discussions. An Ohio university administrator felt it was "important to identify people who were the real thought leaders ... the very best faculty in terms of curricular development" so that when they brought statewide transfer curricula back to their own campuses, "people would respect what they were able to accomplish." A state-level university administrator in Washington specified further: "You have to have key academic people in [each] discipline ... [those] who actually deal with transfer students and know what the transfer patterns look like and the problems students encounter. From our side, it might be associate deans—they tend to be our academic workhorses. From the community college side, it was often a faculty member who taught in the subject or an instruction commission person."

Transfer/Articulation and Admissions/Records Advisory Committees. Articulation officers, transfer directors, advisors, registrars, admissions directors, and similar personnel in both community colleges and universities are—in the words of one Washington higher education official—"an essential piece of the puzzle" in the development of transfer associate degrees, as they understand the intricacies of existing articulation agreements and transfer processes and can identify potential implementation challenges as they arise. Furthermore, they are "the ones who actually have to sell" transfer associate degrees to students. Thus, it is essential to create advisory committees representing these personnel and to ensure clear channels of communication between them and the transfer degree oversight committee. These advisory committees collect and respond to feedback from their colleagues at the district and campus levels, and notify the transfer degree oversight committee of any systemic concerns.

An important finding from our case studies is that while both of these committees are essential to the overall success of implementing transfer associate degrees, the unique perspective members of this group bring often presents a paradox. Members of these committees are essential because they understand the institutional-level details and they are the people who come in direct contact with students, but it is precisely for these reasons—as well as their attachment to local practices and traditions—that they can view potential problems in the process as insurmountable. They offer vital knowledge and expertise; therefore, their administrative concerns should be taken seriously, but local concerns should not be allowed to inhibit creative problem solving or overall progress toward transfer degree implementation.

Communications/Marketing Committee. As several of the chapters in this volume attest (see, in particular, Chapters Four and Eight), a communications/marketing committee that is primarily responsible for informing college and university personnel about the new degrees, raising awareness of new degree pathways among students and their parents, and working with K–12 schools and other organizations to promote the degrees once they are in place is critical and cannot be put into place too soon. Indeed, several interviewees, such as this Ohio community college administrator, lamented overlooking this component of the implementation process: "I think you need a good marketing campaign ... that was one of our downsides: it took us a long time to get the information out. ... We thought this was all great stuff, but the masses really didn't know about it too well." Louisiana's experience, recounted in Chapter Four, echoes this sentiment. An effective marketing or communications plan is thus essential to ensuring that newly developed transfer pathways are utilized by students, and should be considered early in the process of implementing the degrees.

Recognizing the Interests and Values of Constituent Groups to Achieve a Balance Between Autonomy and Efficiency

As the chapters in this volume attest, understanding and recognizing the various perspectives and values of the groups involved in the transfer associate degree implementation process is critical, as the process of implementing transfer associate degrees essentially boils down to a balancing act between the values of autonomy and freedom and those of efficiency, student-centeredness, and the common good. Policymakers, in particular, tend to value the latter over the former, as it can lead to increased system efficiency, cost effectiveness, and theoretically, greater human capital and economic competitiveness. Yet implementation committees in all six states represented in this volume worked hard to preserve their faculty's ability to provide a cutting-edge curriculum, as well as their institutions' freedom to pursue their particular missions and goals, even while asking them to relinquish some control over the lower-division curriculum in order to develop statewide transfer associate degrees.

Key to striking a balance between autonomy and efficiency is understanding the interests and values of each of the major organizational groups involved in systemic transfer and articulation reforms. A New Jersey university administrator argued this point nicely: "The most important thing was to get to the heart of what everybody's really profound concerns were before getting to the nitty-gritty of the little issues, because people often get sidelined on the little stuff, and they don't articulate and confront what they really care about." These values must be articulated and addressed early in the implementation process so that transfer degrees can be developed with them in mind, and so that key actors can work together to find areas where compromise is possible. Most importantly, these concerns must be adequately addressed so that they do not ultimately limit the impact of transfer associate degrees. Figure 9.2 illustrates common interests and values among those involved in systemic transfer and articulation reforms.

To be successful in involving various higher education constituents in the development of transfer associate degrees, different messages must be targeted to different groups. For example, system leaders and administra-

Figure 9.2. Interests and Values of the Major Constituent Groups in Systemic Transfer Reforms

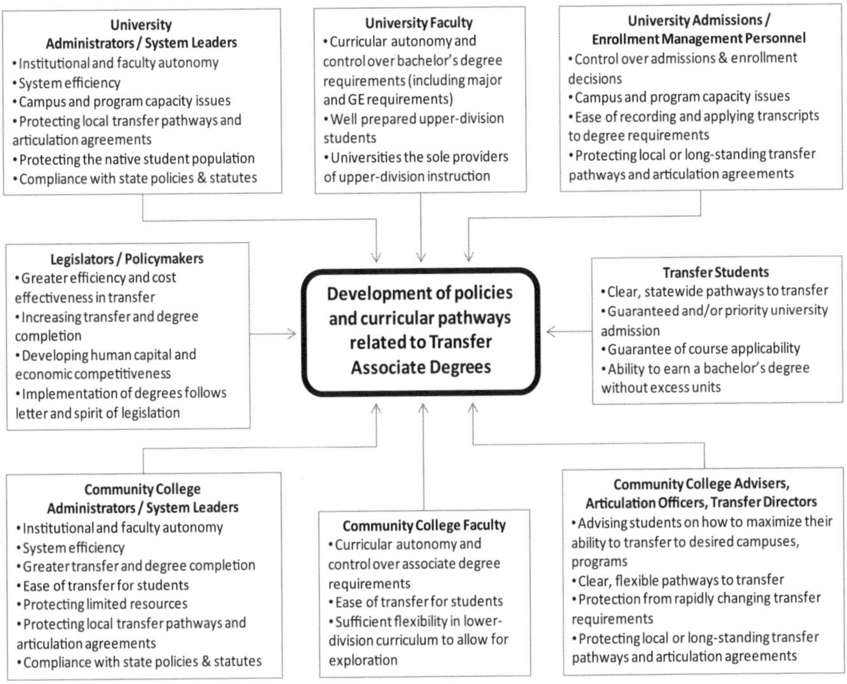

University Administrators / System Leaders
- Institutional and faculty autonomy
- System efficiency
- Campus and program capacity issues
- Protecting local transfer pathways and articulation agreements
- Protecting the native student population
- Compliance with state policies & statutes

University Faculty
- Curricular autonomy and control over bachelor's degree requirements (including major and GE requirements)
- Well prepared upper-division students
- Universities the sole providers of upper-division instruction

University Admissions / Enrollment Management Personnel
- Control over admissions & enrollment decisions
- Campus and program capacity issues
- Ease of recording and applying transcripts to degree requirements
- Protecting local or long-standing transfer pathways and articulation agreements

Legislators / Policymakers
- Greater efficiency and cost effectiveness in transfer
- Increasing transfer and degree completion
- Developing human capital and economic competitiveness
- Implementation of degrees follows letter and spirit of legislation

Development of policies and curricular pathways related to Transfer Associate Degrees

Transfer Students
- Clear, statewide pathways to transfer
- Guaranteed and/or priority university admission
- Guarantee of course applicability
- Ability to earn a bachelor's degree without excess units

Community College Administrators / System Leaders
- Institutional and faculty autonomy
- System efficiency
- Greater transfer and degree completion
- Ease of transfer for students
- Protecting limited resources
- Protecting local transfer pathways and articulation agreements
- Compliance with state policies & statutes

Community College Faculty
- Curricular autonomy and control over associate degree requirements
- Ease of transfer for students
- Sufficient flexibility in lower-division curriculum to allow for exploration

Community College Advisers, Articulation Officers, Transfer Directors
- Advising students on how to maximize their ability to transfer to desired campuses, programs
- Clear, flexible pathways to transfer
- Protection from rapidly changing transfer requirements
- Protecting local or long-standing transfer pathways and articulation agreements

tors may be best persuaded with messages about how transfer associate degrees will reduce excess credits and improve system efficiency. University faculty will likely respond to the notion that they will receive better-prepared students into their programs, while two-year faculty and staff are often motivated by the sense that engaging in this process will lead to improved transfer experiences for their students. Finding the right message to appeal to each group is crucial in ensuring acceptance and involvement in the implementation of transfer associate degrees and other systemic reforms.

Yet bringing these groups to the table is only half of the battle. The next—and arguably harder—step is convincing faculty, administrators, and others to cede some level of autonomy or freedom in order to enact state-wide, student-centered transfer and articulation policies and curricula. Creativity is essential in reaching these compromises, and states will find different ways to balance autonomy and efficiency within their own transfer reforms.

For example, in all six states highlighted in this volume, the universities agreed to accept the community colleges' common general education package as equivalent to their own requirements rather than standardize general education across all colleges and universities in the state. However, although New Jersey universities embraced this idea in principle, and put in place processes by which students can appeal a university's decision about course transferability or applicability to the major, they fought to exclude community colleges from participating in formal appeals processes. In other states, community colleges can initiate appeals processes on behalf of their students. While the desire to maintain autonomy over course transferability and applicability is understandable, a former member of the Arizona transfer and articulation task force explained why community college authority to initiate an appeals process is so important: "Students need to know that if they have a problem they have somebody they can go to ... because a lot of students, especially the ones who are poor or at risk, they may not challenge [the university's ruling]. They just say, 'Oh, I have to take this class over again.' They don't know that there is a system in place." While New Jersey community college administrators would certainly prefer a policy that gave them more latitude to initiate formal appeals, several noted that their attempts to work informally with their university counterparts to resolve specific students' transfer issues had been successful.

Another issue requiring a delicate autonomy/efficiency balancing act has to do with specific institutional requirements that fall outside the parameters (or allotted units) for a transfer associate degree, but that faculty and administrators feel are central to their college's culture or identity. In New Jersey, community colleges were asked to do away with any institutional requirements that would cause a student to earn more than 60 semester credits prior to completing a transfer associate degree. To cope with this diminished autonomy, one college "decided as an institution that we could still support the value of those courses—some students wouldn't take them because they weren't going to fill this particular criteria—but we could still counsel and advise and encourage and value [them]" (New Jersey community college administrator).

In Washington, the four-year institutions were asked to make adjustments to institutional requirements in order to accommodate transfer associate degrees. As a higher education official from that state explained, "One of the ways that we got around the whole issue of prerequisites ... if somebody had a special class that they required, even if it was a 200-level course that they required as a prerequisite, what we asked the university to do was to turn it from a prerequisite into a graduation requirement. So that we weren't trying ... to change their degree requirements, we were just trying to change *when* the student had to take that course." A Washington university administrator offered this advice to those developing transfer associate degrees in other states: "Get creative so you don't have to change your requirements; [you] just figure out how to work around them for students."

In some instances, disciplinary groups in Washington, Arizona, and other states were unable to identify a truly common lower-division transfer pattern that met the requirements for an associate degree—and all of the major prerequisites required by public universities in the state—within a prescribed cap on the number of units. Most often this occurred in disciplines where the universities could not agree amongst themselves as to the best preparation for upper-division study. Although Arizona faculty began by trying to identify at least six common lower-division credits within each equivalent major at the state's three universities, over time universal applicability proved difficult in some disciplines, and educators began instead to develop degree pathways specific to particular universities. The popular Maricopa to ASU Pathways Program (MAPP, described in Chapter Eight)—which was implemented in 2009 and is a prescribed sequence of courses tailored to an Arizona State University major—improves the applicability of courses within a major and protects university autonomy, but does so at the expense of system efficiency.

Similarly, when Washington faculty found it hard to agree on the best preparation for upper-division study in a major, transfer associate degrees were developed with as many common courses as possible, but they also included provisions specifying, for example, that a certain course is required for transfer to University A, but that University B requires a different one. Although the use of stipulations enabled faculty to create transfer associate degrees that are, perhaps, 80 percent common across all institutions, they are less efficient and student-centered than many educators, such as this Washington higher education official, would prefer: "In my opinion, these provisos muddy the waters. And from the advisers' perspective, it makes it really challenging. ... I mean, if you're really trying to create something seamless that keeps options open for students, [provisos must be] kept to an absolute minimum and really have to be strongly justified."

In Ohio, and to some extent in California, Arizona, and New Jersey, the fact that course equivalency is determined by adherence to jointly developed learning outcomes has proven critical to achieving a satisfactory balance between autonomy and lower-division standardization. One New Jersey administrator provided a useful explanation for this phenomenon:

> The underlying issue ... can be articulated fairly concisely. And that is the tendency to say that if you didn't learn it here ... or if you didn't learn it from me, you didn't learn it. ... So when we began to think in terms of learning outcomes as opposed to ... inputs ... the most important thing we learned is that the mind-set changed, and the faculty members began to think in terms of outcomes ... and then the source of the inputs became less important to them.

As demonstrated in Chapter Five, Ohio has instituted a very effective process for determining course equivalency based on learning outcomes. The learning outcomes approach and 70 percent rule are highly valued by Ohio educators as they give faculty "the flexibility of doing things in totally different ways as long as you can show you're addressing those particular outcomes" (Ohio university professor). Furthermore, they focus faculty on the essential competencies required for upper-division study in a major, as well as the curricular structures that are best for students. Basing transfer degrees on common learning outcomes is thus key to creating a system that is, as Ohio educators like to say, both faculty driven and student centered.

While the process of developing transfer associate degrees in various disciplines is not always smooth or easy, the profusion of such degrees in states across the nation prove that—in the words of an Arizona university professor, "if well-educated and considerate representatives from all the campuses get together ... and work it out with input from their own faculties ... compromise is achieved." In other words, while there is no one-size-fits-all model appropriate for all states, it is possible to achieve a balance between autonomy/freedom and efficiency, student-centeredness, and the common good.

Hard Questions for the Future

Thus far, this chapter has demonstrated that with a proper organizational structure and genuine compromise among the values and interests of all involved in the process, transfer associate degrees can be successfully implemented—a narrative repeated and amplified throughout this volume. In this final section, we will look to the future by asking six critical questions relevant to the continued development and success of transfer associate degrees across the country. These questions have been raised both implicitly and explicitly in the volume, but are collected here.

Question 1: **How do we best market newly developed transfer associate degrees to students, parents, faculty, and advisors in order to improve participation rates among community college students?** The lack of statewide efforts to market newly developed transfer associate degrees to students, parents, faculty, and advisors has resulted in, at least in some states, lower-than-expected rates of participation among community college students. As a higher education official in Washington put it, "I think we haven't done a good job in this state of letting people know what the pathways are." As a result, community college students are less aware of available transfer pathways, and do not always understand the benefits of earning a transfer associate degree. All of the states represented in this volume are seeking ways to more effectively promote their statewide transfer pathways; Arizona, for example, has recently created a position for a statewide marketing and communications analyst who will report directly to the intersegmental transfer and articulation oversight committee.

Question 2: **What are the best methods for utilizing technological solutions such as Web-based advising and degree-planning tools, electronic management systems, and/or electronic transcript delivery systems that can be used by all institutions within a state?** In part because of the need to more effectively promote transfer associate degrees, many states are considering and/or implementing technological solutions such as Web-based advising tools for students and staff, electronic management systems that enable faculty review of learning outcomes and course equivalencies, and/or electronic transcript delivery systems that can be used by all institutions. Web-based advising and degree-planning tools, in particular, have emerged as a necessary next step in systemic transfer and articulation reform. See Chapters Five, Six, and Eight for information about technology tools for transfer utilized in Ohio, California, and Arizona.

Question 3: What are the best ways to involve K–12 educators in transfer discussions and/or to think more about how college readiness is and should be related to statewide transfer policies? In recent years, Arizona, Ohio, and New Jersey have begun to involve K–12 educators in transfer conversations and/or think about how college-readiness is and should be related to statewide transfer policies. Chapter Eight discusses Arizona's efforts to address this question in detail. Although some in New Jersey acknowledge a need to similarly "go down into the high schools" (New Jersey policymaker), the state has focused more on creating common definitions of remedial and college-level work. As this state-level community college official explained, "Seeking common ground with the senior colleges on transfer depends in large part on community colleges reaching common ground on important related issues. ... Over the course of two or three years, we got all of our colleges using the same placement tests. ... And we got the colleges to agree to common cut scores." As college-readiness conversations come to the forefront of education policy and practice, other states will likely follow Arizona and New Jersey's lead in incorporating the K–12 sector into statewide transfer and articulation solutions.

Question 4: What are possible solutions to resolving capacity constraints at certain public universities and within popular degree programs? Other than California, few states are currently experiencing capacity issues at universities other than their flagships. Nonetheless, many expect to contend with this issue in the near future and are taking steps to combat the dilemma. For example, educators in Washington are reexamining their 1992 "proportionality agreement," which guarantees that a certain percentage of new enrollment slots at the state's baccalaureate institutions will be set aside for incoming transfer students. California (see Chapter Six), however, already faces severe capacity issues, both at certain public universities and within popular degree programs. Many states across the nation will likely be watching closely to see how California educators are able to deal with these constraints while making significant improvements to its statewide transfer and articulation system.

Question 5: How can we rigorously assess the outcomes of transfer associate degrees over time and utilize those data to strengthen systemic transfer and articulation reforms? Our 2011 study, as well as several of the chapters in this volume, provide early evidence that transfer associate degrees have led to positive outcomes, including greater flexibility and more options for transfer students; improved transfer rates; better preparation for upper-division work; improved degree completion rates; reductions in time and credits to degree; and cost savings for students and states. However, as Chapter Two illustrates, transfer associate degrees and other statewide transfer reforms are relatively new phenomena, and only a few empirical analyses of their outcomes have been conducted (Chapters One, Five, and Eight cite a few of these studies). Furthermore, studies by Anderson, Sun, and Mariana (2006); Falconetti (2009); Roksa and Keith (2008); and Wellman (2002) indicate that the relationship between statewide articulation or transfer policies and improved transfer rates among students is not necessarily clear.

Truly understanding the impact of transfer associate degrees on students and states will require more analyses, conducted over longer periods of time, both within individual states and spanning state boundaries. Empirical evidence that transfer associate degrees are or are not producing the positive outcomes listed above will be critical to the future of these reforms. In particular, evidence of success can be utilized in requests for additional legislative and monetary support, and indications that the degrees are not always working as expected can be used to modify and improve degree pathways to better serve students.

Question 6: How can we best maintain and improve statewide transfer pathways in the current era of reduced funding for public higher education? Although several states had implemented the primary components of their transfer associate degrees prior to the Great Recession, others such as Louisiana did so in the midst of the fiscal crisis (see Chapter Four). And in all states, budget cuts and resource constraints continue to threaten the success of these reforms. In the words of an Ohio university administrator, "The state has funded this at $2.5 million. Now that is in great jeopardy, and what we've been putting together is an alternative funding model ... I think how we continue to fund this and enhance the funding is going to be a great challenge." Budget cuts not only jeopardize funding for intersegmental disciplinary meetings and overall transfer coordination and oversight, but they may have more indirect effects as well:

> One of the things that has happened is that the state universities have gotten bigger budget cuts of state funds than community colleges. ... That makes them a little less generous toward community college faculty and community college courses. And so their willingness to try to figure out how—or to compromise around their course requirements, what they require for majors, what they will or will not accept—is going down. ... I think that is a trickle-down effect of the tight budget situation. (Washington state-level community college administrator)

Reduced funding is a clear and undeniable challenge. States will have to find ways to maintain and improve statewide transfer pathways in the current era of reduced funding for public higher education. Hopefully, the promise that transfer associate degrees hold for improving system efficiency and generating cost savings is enough to keep policymakers and educators invested in current reforms and supportive of the next steps.

References

Anderson, G., Sun, J. C., and Mariana, A. "Effectiveness of Statewide Articulation Agreements on the Probability of Transfer: A Preliminary Policy Analysis." *Review of Higher Education,* 2006, 29(3), 261–291.

Falconetti, A. M. G. "2 + 2 Statewide Articulation Policy, Student Persistence, and Success in Florida Universities." *Community College Journal of Research and Practice,* 2009, 33, 238–255.

Kisker, C. B., Wagoner, R. L., and Cohen, A. M. *Implementing Statewide Transfer & Articulation Reform: An Analysis of Transfer Associate Degrees in Four States.* Los Angeles: Center for the Study of Community Colleges, 2011.

Roksa, J., and Keith, B. "Credits, Time, and Attainment: Articulation Policies and Success After Transfer." *Educational Evaluation and Policy Analysis,* 2008, 30(3), 236–254.

Wellman, J. V. *State Policy and Community College-Baccalaureate Transfer* (National Center report no. 02-6). San Jose, Calif.: National Center for Public Policy and Higher Education and Institute for Higher Education Policy, 2002.

RICHARD L. WAGONER *is assistant professor of higher education at the University of California, Los Angeles, and a director of the Center for the Study of Community Colleges.*

CARRIE B. KISKER *is an education research and policy consultant in Los Angeles, California, as well as a director of the Center for the Study of Community Colleges.*

10

This chapter provides an annotated bibliography of articles about the effects of transfer associate degrees and related statewide transfer and articulation policies. It also provides links to transfer degree legislation in several states.

Sources and Information on Transfer Associate Degrees

Carlos Ayon

Effects of Transfer Associate Degrees and Related Statewide Transfer and Articulation Policies

The following articles examine the effects of transfer associate degrees and other statewide transfer and articulation policies on students and states.

> Anderson, G., Sun, J. C., and Mariana, A. "Effectiveness of Statewide Articulation Agreements on the Probability of Transfer: A Preliminary Policy Analysis." *Review of Higher Education*, 2006, 29(3), 261–291.

In this article, the authors seek to uncover whether there is a difference in transfer rates between states with articulation agreements and those without such mandates. Additionally, they seek to identify other factors impacting the probability of transferring, arguing that individual student characteristics can inform policymakers of alternative or supplemental initiatives to increase transfer rates. The authors found no significant difference in the transfer rates of students in states with statewide articulation agreements relative to those without such agreements.

> Falconetti, A. M. G. "2 + 2 Statewide Articulation Policy, Student Persistence, and Success in Florida Universities." *Community College Journal of Research and Practice*, 2009, 33, 238–255.

This study examined the continued viability of Florida's 2 + 2 articulation agreement by comparing the academic success and persistence among Florida public community college graduates and native juniors at three universities. The results revealed that transfer students graduated with fewer cumulative credit hours than native students, and that there was no significant difference in the final grade point averages of the two groups of students. However, transfer students were more likely to leave college prior to graduation. The author concludes that transfer students are academically competitive but would benefit from student services and programs focused on retention and student engagement.

> Goff, D. G. "A Descriptive Study of the Associate in Science and Associate in Applied Science Degree General Education Modules for Articulation and Transfer in Maryland and Florida." Unpublished manuscript, 2003. (ED47683)

Both Florida and Maryland have instituted statewide policies meant to drive high levels of transfer between two- and four-year institutions. This paper compares the articulation and transfer policies in these two states, examining how state governance structures impact articulation and transfer.

> Kisker, C. B., Wagoner, R. L., and Cohen, A. M. *Implementing Statewide Transfer & Articulation Reform: An Analysis of Transfer Associate Degrees in Four States*. Los Angeles: Center for the Study of Community Colleges, 2011.

This study was the impetus for this volume of *New Directions for Community Colleges*. It examines the development of transfer associate degrees in Arizona, New Jersey, Ohio, and Washington, and identifies the strategies used to implement them in each state. The authors also provide recommendations to guide systemic transfer and articulation reforms in other states.

> Roksa, J., and Keith, B. "Credits, Time, and Attainment: Articulation Policies and Success After Transfer." *Educational Evaluation and Policy Analysis*, 2008, 30(3), 236–254.

Based on a historical review of state legislation, the authors propose that articulation policies do not improve transfer rates because that is not their intended purpose. They argue the main goal of articulation policies is to prevent the loss of credits when students transfer within state higher education systems. The authors discuss the limitations of existing data and propose that future studies be designed to specifically evaluate the transfer or loss of credits applicable toward general education requirements.

Wellman, J. V. *State Policy and Community College-Baccalaureate Transfer* (National Center report no. 02-6). San Jose, Calif.: National Center for Public Policy and Higher Education and Institute for Higher Education Policy, 2002.

This report examines two- to four-year transfer state policies in six states—Arkansas, Florida, New Mexico, New York, North Carolina, and Texas—describing how each of the states uses policy to affect transfer performance by focusing on governance, enrollment planning, academic policies affecting transfer, and data collection and accountability. The report demonstrates that there is not much difference between high-performing and low-performing states' approaches to basic transfer policy. High-performing states had stronger statewide governance capacities, whereas low-performing states relied on institutional governance structures and, presumably, voluntary collaborations. All of the states in the analysis fell short of fully utilizing state policy tools to maximize transfer. The paper concludes with policy recommendations for invigorating two- to four-year transfer.

Transfer Associate Degree Legislation and Policies

The following section provides links to policies and legislation pertaining to transfer associate degrees in various states.

Arizona. In 1996, Arizona's legislature included the following language in the appropriations for both the state's community colleges and universities (Arizona Board of Regents and State Board of Directors for Community Colleges, 1996, p. 1):

> The Arizona board of regents (ABOR) and the state board of directors for community colleges (state board) shall jointly establish a study committee comprised of university and community college members who are representatives of faculty, academic administration, student services and the chief executive officers. It is the intent of the legislature that this study committee establish a seamless statewide articulation and transfer system, including the process for transfer of lower division general education credits and curriculum requirements for majors, with the objective of reaching consensus on an agreement that assures that community college students may transfer to Arizona public universities without loss of credit towards a baccalaureate degree. The ABOR and the state board shall present the agreement for review by the joint legislative budget committee by December 15, 1996.

Information about Arizona's transfer associate degrees, the Arizona General Education Curriculum, and other statewide transfer and articulation tools can be found at www.aztransfer.com/aztransfer/index.html. Chapter Eight in this volume describes many of these transfer programs and tools in detail.

California. California's transfer associate degrees were set in motion by Senate Bill 1440, authored by Senator Padilla in 2010. The full text of the bill can be accessed at www.sb1440.org/Portals/4/sb1440home/Policy/sb_1440_bill_20100929_chaptered.pdf. Chapter Six details the implementation of SB 1440 in California.

Florida. Florida has a long history of strong articulation between two- and four-year institutions: any student that completes an associate degree is guaranteed admission into a public university degree program, with all of the core course units transferring as a block to the public institution. Additional information about transfer and transfer degrees within the State University System of Florida can be found at www.flbog.edu/forstudents/ati/transfer.php.

Louisiana. Louisiana's Act 356 resulted in the establishment of statewide transfer associate degrees in that state. Detailed information on Louisiana's Transfer Degree Guarantee can be found at www.latransferdegree.org/index.html, and the full text of Act 356 can be accessed at http://legis.state.la.us/billdata/streamdocument.asp?did=449955. Chapter Four in this volume presents a narrative account of the process of developing Louisiana's Transfer Degree Guarantee.

New Jersey. Chapter 175 of the New Jersey Statutes, otherwise known as "The Lampitt Bill" (see Chapter Seven), mandated the creation of transfer associate degrees in that state. The Lampitt Bill can be found at www.njleg.state.nj.us/2006/Bills/PL07/175_.PDF. Following passage of this bill, New Jersey's Presidents' Council adopted the Comprehensive Statewide Transfer Agreement, which details the transfer and application of credits from community colleges to public baccalaureate-granting institutions. The Agreement can be accessed at www.nj.gov/highereducation/PDFs/XferAgreementOct08.pdf.

North Carolina. The North Carolina Comprehensive Articulation Agreement (www.nccommunitycolleges.edu/programs/comprehensive_a_a.htm) governs the transfer of credits between the state's community colleges and public universities, and has as its objective the smooth transfer of students.

Ohio. In 1990, the Ohio Board of Regents adopted the Ohio Articulation and Transfer Policy (http://regents.ohio.gov/transfer/policy/index.php), which established the principles of equitable treatment among transfer and native students, encouraged associate degree completion prior to transfer, and led to the creation of the Ohio Transfer Module (OTM). Thirteen years later, the legislature passed House Bill 95 (http://regents.ohio.gov/transfer/policy/appendixA.php#95), which mandated the development of Transfer Assurance Guides (TAGS). In 2005, the legislature passed House Bill 66 (http://regents.ohio.gov/transfer/policy/transfer_policy_HB66.php), which extended the OTM and TAGs to certain technical or applied fields. Ohio's transfer and articulation system is discussed in detail in Chapter Five.

Washington. As Chapter Three details, Washington State's transfer process has been in existence for over 40 years. Information about the state's transfer associate degrees can be found at www.sbctc.edu/college/_e-transferdegrees.aspx. The Washington Student Achievement Council provides detailed information about these degrees, as well as links to various related policy documents. This information can be accessed at www.wsac.wa.gov/PreparingForCollege/AdmissionsAndTransfer/Pathways.

References

Arizona Board of Regents and State Board of Directors for Community Colleges. *Report of the Transfer Articulation Task Force.* Phoenix, Ariz.: Authors, 1996.

CARLOS AYON is a graduate student in higher education at the University of California, Los Angeles.

INDEX

AA-T. *See* Associate in arts for transfer degree (AA-T)
Academic Program Articulation Steering Committee (APASC; Arizona), 79–82, 84, 86–89; Consortium for Transfer and Alignment (ACTA), 80–81, 85, 87
ACTA. *See* Academic Program Articulation Steering Committee (APASC; Arizona); Consortium for Transfer and Alignment
Advanced Placement, 46, 53
AGEC. *See* Arizona; General Education Curriculum (AGEC)
Alexandria, Louisiana, 36
Anderson, G., 91, 102, 105
Andreas, M., 2, 17
APASC. *See* Academic Program Articulation Steering Committee (APASC; Arizona)
Arizona, 3, 5–9, 14, 94, 99, 106; Career Information System (AzCIS), 86; Department of Education, 81, 86; developing culture of transfer and student success in, 79–89; General Education Curriculum (AGEC), 81–83, 86, 87, 107; Joint Council of Presidents (JCP), 79–80, 84; Legislature (ARS 15–1824), 81, 83–84; Senate Bill 1186, 83–84; Shared Numbering Steering Committee (SC), 84; Shared Numbering System Committee (SNSC), 83–84; State Board of Directors for Community Colleges, 79, 107; State Board of Regents (ABOR), 79–81, 84, 87, 107; State Longitudinal Database System, 86; State System for Information on Student Transfer (ASSIST), 86–87; transfer associate degrees legislation and policies in, 107; transfer degrees in, 82
Arizona State University (ASU), 82–83, 99
Arizona Transfer model, 86; and Academic Curriculum Review and Evaluation System (ACRES), 86; and Arizona Course Equivalency Tracking System (ACETS), 86; and Arizona General Education Curriculum (AGEC), 81–83; ATF Chatlines, 86–87; challenges ahead for, 88–889; Course Equivalency Guide (CEG), 86; and discipline-specific Articulation Task Forces (ATFs), 80, 87, 88, 94; and Education and Career Action Plans system (ECAP), 86; and importance of institutional collaborations in improving transfer, 85; infrastructure of, 79–81; lessons learned from, 87–88; and Maricopa to ASU Pathways Program (MAPP), 82–83, 85, 99; and shared course numbering system, 83–84; technology tools for, 85–87; Transfer Admission Guarantees (TAGs) in, 83; and Transfer Articulation Task Force (TATF), 81–82; and Transfer Associate Degrees, 81–83
ASSIST (Articulation System Stimulating Intersegmental Transfer; California), 56, 57, 61
Associate degrees for transfer: and California's Course Identification Numbering (C-ID) System, 60–63; and creating and documenting processes for developing degrees, 67; and ensuring clear communication, 66–67; and ensuring faculty-driven approach and utilizing existing transfer infrastructure in implementing, 65–66; and establishing universal buy-in as goal, 66; overcoming (most) challenges in implementing, 64–65
Associate in arts for transfer degree (AA-T), 59, 61–66
Associate in science for transfer (AS-T) degree, 22–24, 59, 61–63, 65, 66; guidelines for (Washington State), 26
AS-T. *See* Associate of science for transfer degree
Ayon, C., 3, 105
AZTransfer.com, 85–86, 107

Baccalaureate Associate Colleges, 14–15
Berkeley, California, 13
Big Ideas Project (New Jersey), 69–70
Bill & Melinda Gates Foundation, 7
Bloom, B., 15
Bringing Down the Silos (Tafel), 47
Budget cuts, effect of, 102–103

111

California, 2–3, 7–9, 13, 14, 99, 101; Articulation Numbering System, 60; Assembley Bill 2302, 58; call for associate degrees for transfer in, 55–58; Course Identification Numbering System (C-ID), 60; faculty reflections on implementing associate degrees for transfer in, 55–68; legislation and policies regarding transfer associate degrees, 108; Legislative Analyst's Office, 65; Senate Bill 1440, 55–68, 93, 108

California Community Colleges, 6, 55, 56, 59, 61–67; Academic Senate for, 60, 63, 64; Chancellor's Office, 62, 63; faculty, 59

California State University (CSU) system, 6, 55, 56, 58, 59, 61–67; GE-Breadth, 61

Campaign for College Opportunity (California), 6

Capacity constraints, 101

Career Technical Credit Transfer (CTAGs), 46, 48–51, 53, 54

Career Technical Education fields, 59

Carnegie Classification System, 14–15

Carnevale, A., 69

CEMS. *See* Course Equivalency Management System (CEMS)

Center for the Study of Community Colleges (California), 56

C-ID. *See* California); Course Identification Numbering System (C-ID

Cohen, A. M., 1, 2, 5, 7, 13, 17, 56, 58, 70, 76, 91, 106

College Board, 46

Community Colleges Act (Washington State Legislature), 20

Complete College America, 63, 64

Comprehensive State-Wide Transfer Agreement, 9

Compton, P., 2, 6, 45

COP. *See* Council of Presidents (COP; Washington State)

Cope, K. L., 2, 31

Council of Presidents (COP; Washington State), 18, 22

Course Equivalency Management System (CEMS), 53

Course Identification Numbering System (C-ID; California), 60–64; associate degrees for transfer and, 60

Crabill, K., 3, 69

"Credits, Time, and Attainment: Articulation Policies and Success after Transfer" *(Educational Evaluation and Policy Analysis)*, 106

"Descriptive Study of the Associate in Science and Associate in Applied Science Degree General Education Modules for Articulation and Transfer in Maryland and Florida" (Goff), 106

Direct transfer agreement degree (DTA), 21–23, 25, 26

DTA. *See* Direct transfer agreement degree (DTA)

"Effectiveness of Statewide Articulation Agreements on the Probability of Transfer: A Preliminary Policy Analysis" *(Review of Higher Education)*, 105

Equivalency, concept of, 48

Eunice, Louisiana, 34

Everett High School (Washington), 20

Faculty Discipline Review Group (FDRG; California), 61–63

Falconetti, A.M.G., 102, 105

Florida, 7, 105–106, 108; State University System, 108

Fong, P., 58

Fresno, California, 13

Getting AHEAD: Access to Higher Education and Degrees (Arizona), 85

Glenn, D., 6

Goff, D. G., 106

Great Recession, 102–103

Gustafson, R., 2, 45

Harper-Marinick, M., 3, 79

HBCUs (historically black colleges and universities), 42

Hezel Associates, 5–6, 82, 89

Higher Education Coordinating Board (HECB; Washington State), 18

ICRC. *See* Intercollege Relations Commission (ICRC; Washington State)

ICW. *See* Independent Colleges of Washington (ICW)

IGETC, 61

Implementing Statewide Transfer & Articulation Reform (Kisker, Wagoner, and Cohen), 106

"Implementing Statewide Transfer & Articulation Reform: An Analysis of Gransfer Associate Degrees in Four

States" (Kisker, Wagoner, and Cohen), 7
Independent Colleges of Washington (ICW), 18–20
Intercollege Relations Commission (ICRC; Washington State), 18–21, 23
Interinstitutional Committee of Academic Officers (ICAO), 20
Intersegmental Committee of the Academic Senates (ICAS; California), 66
Intersegmental Curriculum Workgroup, 59, 62

Jensen, C., 1
Joint Transfer Council (JTC; Washinjgton State), 17–20, 23–25
Joliet Junior College, 13
JTC. *See* Joint Transfer Council (JTC; Washington State)

K-12 educators, 101
Kansas, 14
Keith, B., 7, 102, 106
Kisker, C. B., 1–3, 5, 7, 17, 56, 58, 70, 76, 91, 106
KnowHow2Go portal, 86

LAICU. *See* Louisiana Association of Independent Colleges and Universities (LAICU)
Lampitt Bill (New Jersey Assemby Bill 3968), 72–77, 108; laying groundwork for, 71–72
Law, J., 2, 45
Louisiana, 7, 8, 108; Act 356, 32, 108; Board of Regents, 35–39, 43; Statewide Articulation and Transfer Council, 33, 35–37
Louisiana Association of Independent Colleges and Universities (LAICU), 42
Louisiana Community and Technical College System (LCTCS), 37
Louisiana State University (LSU) System, 34, 35, 37
Louisiana Transfer Degree Guarantee, 2, 40, 108; and audience for articulation, 40–43; and General Education (GE) as common transfer currency of unmeasured value, 37–40; and helpful haste and inventive itinerancy, 32–34; and prestige paradox, 34–37; and short road to success, 31–44

Maliszewski, C., 3, 69
Mariana, A., 102, 105

Maricopa Community College District (Arizona), 82–84
Maryland, 106
Miami University (Ohio), 53
Moore, C., 1
Mustafa, C. B., 6

National Student Clearinghouse, 14
Nespoli, L., 3, 69
New Directions for Community Colleges, 3, 106
New Jersey, 3, 7, 8, 10, 69–77, 98, 106, 108; Commission on Higher Education, 72; Office of Higher Education, 72; Statutes, Chapter 175, 72
New Jersey community college transfer experience: and Assemby Bill 3968 ("Lampitt Bill"), 71, 108; future of, 76–77; and identifying early-major pathways, 77; importance of New Jersey President's Council in facilitating implementation of, 73–75; and involving faculty, 77; role of presidential leadership in, 69–77; and strengthening data collection, 77
New Jersey Comprehensive State-Wide Transfer Agreement, 9, 108
New Jersey Council of County Colleges, 69–70
New Jersey Legislature, 71, 72
New Jersey Presidents' Council, 10, 76, 108; importance of, in facilitating implementation, 73–75; Transfer Committee, 74–76
New York, 14
NJ STARS II scholarship, 71
NJ STARS scholarship, 71
NJ Transfer Web site, 72
North Carolina, 7; Comprehensive Articulation Agreement, 108
Northland Pioneer College (NPC; Arizona), 83

Obama administration, 6
Ohio, 2, 6–9, 45–54, 94–96, 99–100, 106, 108; Department of Education, 46, 47; General Assembly, 46, 52; House Bill 66, 108; House Bill 95, 108; Revised Code, 50
Ohio Articulation and Transfer Network (OATN), 48, 53
Ohio Articulation and Transfer Policy, 9–10, 46–47, 49 Fig. 5.1, 108; hallmarks of, 52–54

Ohio Board of Regents (OBR), 6, 9–10, 46–48, 50, 52, 53, 108
Ohio Transfer Mobility System: and establishing course equivalency, 48–51; evolution of, 45–54; and faculty-determined course equivelency, 45–54; and statewide structure of collaboration, 51–52
Ohio Transfer Module (OTM), 45–47, 51, 53, 108
Oregon, 7, 14
OTM. *See* Ohio Transfer Module (OTM)
Outcomes, 101–102

Padilla, A., 55, 108
Participation rates, improving, 100
Patton, J., 2–3, 55
Pavelcheck, D., 5–6
Pennsylvania, 14
Pilati, M., 2–3, 55
Pima Community College District (Arizona), 84
Pitman, K., 5–6
Portland State University, 43

Reforming the State's Transfer Process: A Progress Report on Senate Bill 1440 (California Legislative Analyst's Office), 65
Roksa, J., 7, 102, 106

SB 1440. *See* California); Student Transfer Achievement Reform Act (SB 1440, Padilla
SBCTC. *See* State Board for Community and Technical Colleges (SBCTC; Washington)
Schwarzenegger, A., 55
Shared unique number (SUN), 84
Sherman, J., 2, 17
Shulock, N., 1
Smith, N., 69
South Carolina, 7
Southern University System, 35
State Board for Community and Technical Colleges (SBCTC; Washington), 19, 20, 22, 23, 25
State Board of Directors for Community Colleges of Arizona, 81–82
State of New Jersey Higher Education, 70
State Policy and Community College-Baccalauriate Transfer (Wellman), 107

STEM (science, technology, engineering, and math) fields, 22–23, 42, 59
Stern, P., 5–6
Strohl, J., 69
Student Transfer Achievement Reform Act (SB 1440, Padilla; California), 55–57, 59, 60, 65–68; Implementation Oversight Committee, 59, 64, 65, 93–94; and Intersegmental Curriculum Workgroup, 59, 62; lessons learned from implementation of, 65–67; and setting stage for success, 58; Transfer Model Curricula as key to coordinated implementation of, 61; and what could have happened in response to, (and what did), 58–59
Sun, J. C., 102, 105
Swarthout, J., 3, 79
Systematic transfer reforms, interests and values of major constituent groups in, 97 Fig. 9.2
Szelenyi, K., 6

Tafel, J., 2, 45, 47
TAGs. *See* Arizona); New Jersey); Ohio); Transfer Admission Guarantees (TAGs; Transfer Assurance Guides (TAGs; Tuition Aid Grants (TAGs
Technological solutions, 100–101
Texas, 7, 14
Transfer Admission Guarantees (TAGs; Arizona), 83, 85
Transfer associate degrees, 1; and acceptance policy for upper-division courses, 9–10; and associate and/or bachelor's degree credit limits, 9; and common general education pattern, 8; and common lower-division premajor and early-major pathways, 8; and communications/marketing committee, 95–96; and curricular oversight and faculty disciplinary committees, 94–95; elements of effective, 5–10; and focus on credit applicability, 8; and guaranteed and/or priority university admission, 9; hard questions for the future regarding, 100–103; historical context for, 13–16; ideal state-level organizational structure for, 92–96; and junior status upon transfer, 8–9; legislation and policies, 107–109; model organizational structure for implementing, 92 Fig. 9.1; in perspective, 91–103; and recognizing

interests and values of constituent groups to achieve balance between autonomy and efficiency, 96–100; sources and information on, 105–109; and transfer degree oversight committee, 93–94; and transfer/articulation and admissions/records advisory committees, 95

Transfer Assurance Guides (TAGs; Ohio), 45–51, 53, 54, 108

Transfer Model Curricula (TMC; California), 61, 65, 67; and degree development and approval process, 61–64; and Faculty Discipline Review Group (FDRG), 61–62; finalized for use, 62–63; as key to coordinated implementation of SB 1440, 61; status of, and degree development, 63–64; vetting of, 62

Transfer structure (Washington state), 17–28

Transfer Student Bill of Rights, 25

Transfer Student Rights and Responsibilities (Washington State), 25–26

Transfer Task Force (California), 56

Tuition Aid Grants (TAGs; New Jersey), 71

"2+2 Statewide Articulation Policy, Student Persistence, and Success in Florida Universities" (*Community College Journal of Research and Practice*), 105

Umbrella Policy (Washington Council for High School-College Relations), 21

University of California system, 56, 58, 66

University of Chicago, 13

University of Louisiana System, 34

University of Wisconsin, Milwaukee, 43

University System of Ohio (USO), 46–51, 53

Wagoner, R. I., 1–3, 5, 7, 17, 56, 58, 70, 76, 91, 106

Walter S. Johnson Foundation, 7

Washington Association of Community and Technical Colleges (WACTC), 19

Washington Association of Community College Presidents, 20

Washington Council for High School-College Relations (WCHSCR), 18–21

Washington Higher Education Coordination Board, 6

Washington State, 2, 5–9, 94, 99, 109; forty years of direct transfer in, 20–25; future possibilities in, 27–28; and growing numbers of transfer students (crucial event 1), 20–21; higher education sector groups in, 19–20; and how to best prepare STEM transfer students (crucial event 4), 22–23; and how to improve transfer in high-demand majors (crucial event 6), 24–25; and how to maintain current agreements (crucial event 5), 23–24; and Intercollege Relations Commissionm, 18–19; and Joint Transfer Council, 17–18; Legislature, 20; and legislature threatens intervention (crucial event 2), 21; lessons learned in, 28; major players in transfer structure in, 17–20; more recent policies to improve transfer in, 25–27; process used to approve, implement, and monitor transfer policy in, 24; secrets to successful transfer model in, 27; State Board for Community and Technical Colleges (SBCTC), 18; successful transfer structure in, 17–28; transfer liaison, 26; and will transfer students have place to transfer to (crucial event 3), 22

Washington Student Achievement Council (WSAC), 18, 19, 21, 22, 25, 26, 109

Wellman, J. V., 102, 107

Western Governor's University, Washington, 19

What Councelors Need to Know about AA-T, AS-T Degrees (California Community Colleges Chancellor's Office), 66

WSAC. *See* Washington Student Achievement Council

Wyoming, 14

LB	Implementing transfer
2360	associate degrees:
.I565	perspectives from
2013	the state.

JOSSEY-BASS
A Wiley Brand

INSIDE HIGHER ED
insidehighered.com

GAYLORD